Introduction

It would be wrong to suggest that Labour's term of office has been a catalogue of failure; that nothing good has come of the last twelve years. Indeed, when one considers Labour's record, it is clear that some tremendous things were achieved, such as civil partnerships and devolution. But it's equally clear that Labour's record falls far below the promise of 1997 and that in all too many ways the people of Britain have been let down.

Despite proclaiming their commitment to 'education, education, education', Labour have delivered an education system that sees almost 40 per cent of eleven-year-olds failing to meet the government's own reading standard and only 13 per cent of children eligible for free school meals achieving the benchmark five GCSEs. Despite promising a better health service for all and doubling NHS funding to see that goal achieved, Labour have actually managed to deliver a 2.5 per cent reduction in NHS productivity year on year. Despite taking the country into Iraq and Afghanistan, Labour have failed to provide our troops with the equipment they need to get the job done. Despite pledging to be 'tough on crime and tough on the causes of crime', the last twelve years have seen violent crime almost double and gun crime quadruple. Despite promising and end an 'end to boom and bust', Labour have presided over the worst recession in living memory. And despite promising that the UK would lead the world out of that recession, Labour's policy of reckless borrowing ensured that the UK was the last country of the G20 to emerge from recession.

Alongside these failures, though, the British people have had to contend with a culture of dishonesty: a culture in which it was OK to promise the British people a referendum on the EU constitution only to renege on that promise when it looked like the British people might not give Labour the result they wanted; a culture which said it was OK to label the opposition leader as 'Mr 10 per cent' when all the while Labour were themselves planning 10 per cent public spending cuts of their own; and a culture that said it was OK to tell the people of Hartlepool in advance of a by-election that their maternity ward was safe from cuts only to turn around and close that maternity ward when the by-election was over.

It is time for the failure and the dishonesty to come to an end. And it's time to take the country in a fresh direction that better reflects the values and aspirations of the British people. Thankfully, an opportunity to achieve just that is within sight. Gordon Brown can delay it no longer; a general election is fast approaching. And in that general election the British people will have a clear choice: vote for a Labour Party that has proved itself all too incapable, or a Conservative Party that – as the many chapters of this book demonstrate – has a robust and dynamic plan to take Britain in a new direction, a direction with better healthcare, better education, better policing, a strong economy, lower unemployment and a greener environment.

Principles and philosophy of the modern Conservative Party

David Cameron's victory in the contest to become leader of the Conservative Party was secured on a platform of radical change. And change the party he has, from its logo to its now irrefutable commitment to the NHS. Under Cameron, the Conservatives have genuinely transformed into a party that truly reflects the values and aspirations of modern Britain. But what are the principles and philosophy that underpin the modern Conservative Party's approach to government?

Empowering and informing people

The central philosophy of the modern Conservative Party is the belief that, as David Cameron outlined in a June 2009 speech, there is a need for a fundamental change in 'the balance of power between the citizen and the state so that ultimately it's people in control of their government, not the other way round'. This instinctive desire to give people more power over their own lives isn't an absolute argument against the role of the state; rather, in part, it's a recognition that decisions are ultimately much better when they are taken as closely to the person or people affected as possible, and when the people affected have the power to hold the decision maker to account. This philosophy manifests in a number of principles:

1. Where decision-making power can be devolved to the individual citizen it should be. For example, see the Schools chapter for the Conservatives' commitment to giving parents the power to set up their own schools.

2. Where decision-making can't be devolved to the individual citizen it should be devolved as closely as possible to those who would be affected by that decision. For example, see the Countryside chapter for the Conservatives' commitment to giving local councils rather than central government the power to decide how many new houses should be built in their area.

3. Whenever a decision is taken, the person or organisation taking that decision should be accountable to the people affected by it. For example, see the Crime chapter, which discusses the Conservative commitment to creating elected police commissioners so that local people would be able to hold their local police force to account.

4. If decision-making power is the be devolved in this way then people must have the access to the kind of information and data they need to make the relevant decision for themselves or to hold the relevant-decision maker to account. The Conservative Party recognises that it's not enough to simply empower people to start their own school or to create a police commissioner. If people are going to be able to exercise their new-found power effectively they need access to the kind of data that will enable them to make an informed decision. This means granting people unprecedented access to data held by public bodies. To return to police commissioners, for example, a Conservative government would require police forces to publish a crime map detailing incidences of crime at a street-by-street level.

As a second element of this philosophy, we believe that the accumulation of massive power by the state over people's lives goes against the civil liberties which form the foundation of British liberal democracy. This is covered in more detail in the Civil Liberties chapter. But suffice to say, when it comes to government the

Conservative Party will be guided by one principle: the database state and surveillance society which has grown up under Labour must be massively scaled back.

Taking a multi-dimensional approach

The modern Conservative Party is committed to the philosophy that, with regard to the role of the state, there are very few problems which do not require multi-dimensional responses. So whereas some look at a problem like crime and see it purely as a criminal justice issue, the Conservative Party sees it as a problem that extends into its policies on the family, education, health, welfare and beyond. Accordingly, when tackling any problem, from unemployment to terrorism, a Conservative government would be guided by the principle that linkages between different policy areas must be identified and exploited in order to achieve a satisfactory solution.

Tackling root causes

Closely tied to the belief that most problems require a multi-dimensional response is the idea that problems only ever get solved if you tackle their root causes. So whereas the Labour approach has all too often been to treat a problem only once it has occurred, the Conservative Party is driven by the principle that prevention is better than cure.

Outcomes count

One final aspect of modern Conservative philosophy that should be mentioned is the belief that you can only solve problems if you focus on outcomes. The example given above of crime-mapping is one indication of how a Conservative government would ensure that public service providers have their mind constantly on the outcomes they are trying to achieve, but another principle that would guide this philosophy must also be mentioned: payment by results.

Under a Conservative government public service providers, such as back-to-work programmes, would only be paid according to the results they achieve.

The economy

That Britain was the last country in the G20 to leave recession speaks volumes about the state of the UK economy. Whereas Gordon Brown promised an 'end to boom and bust', we have found that his actions as Chancellor and then as Prime Minister served only to prolong and deepen the bust when it inevitably arrived. From borrowing on an unprecedented scale (UK debt has doubled in the last five years alone) to failing to fix the roof when the sun was shining, Brown ensured that when facing the worst economic crisis in living memory our capability and resilience were severely limited.

It's clear that to get Britain back on track the deficit has to be cut dramatically. But whilst cutting the deficit – a challenge which is discussed at length in the Tax and Spend chapter – is critically important, it doesn't go to the heart of the problem. The deeper issue is how we prevent ourselves from getting into a similar situation in the future.

In addressing this issue there are two fundamental questions which must be answered. The first is how to ensure that future British governments will both live within their means and put money aside in the good years for use in the bad years, i.e. how to ensure fiscal responsibility. The second is how to better protect against the kind of collapse in the financial sector which delivered us into recession into the first place.

Delivering fiscal responsibility

Gordon Brown proclaimed that a Labour government could guarantee fiscal responsibility by employing fiscal rules, the most important of which were the 'Golden Rule' and the 'Sustainable Investment Rule'. The former requires that the current budget balances over the economic cycle and the latter requires that each year net government debt does not exceed 40 per cent of GDP. However, it has become all too apparent that these rules have failed utterly to achieve their objective. The Golden Rule proved to be woefully malleable; indeed on two occasions when Brown was Chancellor he simply opted to change the start and end date of the economic cycle when the rule was about to be broken. Clearly, any rule which allows for this kind of flexibility isn't worth the paper it's written on. And as for the Sustainable Investment Rule, its record would be laughable were it not so tragic. Even allowing for the fact that the rule conveniently excludes large portions of government debt from the calculation of net debt, the UK's net debt stood at 49.3 per cent of GDP at the end of September 2009 (according to the Office of National Statistics). And if you include financial interventions in the net debt calculation it stands at a tremendous 60.2 per cent of GDP (as at the end of November 2009).

But even such shoddy rules don't go the whole way in explaining why fiscal irresponsibility – through, for example, the accumulation of massive debt – took hold during Labour's tenure. To understand that, one simply has to consider the Treasury's record with fiscal forecasts. As the policy paper *Reconstruction: Our Plan for a Strong Economy* points out, the Treasury has been consistently 'over-optimistic in its fiscal forecasts'. For example, in every Budget since 2001 the Treasury's balance forecast has been utterly wrong;

with the actual budget balance turning out to be worse on each occasion. Moreover, each Budget has consistently predicted that a surplus would be achieved in two to three years, yet such a surplus has yet to materialise. We shouldn't be surprised that Budgets, and the Treasury more generally, tend to be overly optimistic; after all, they're both controlled by whichever party is in government. But the net result is all too clear: by painting a picture of economic health and creating the impression that surpluses are just around the corner, the Treasury's projections only serve to encourage ever higher rates of borrowing.

The lessons from this are obvious. Firstly, fiscal rules cannot be trusted to deliver fiscal responsibility and secondly, politically influenced fiscal projections from the Treasury only serve to encourage fiscal irresponsibility.

With that in mind, the Conservative Party has committed to a fundamentally different approach to ensuring fiscal responsibility, removing political influence from official fiscal forecasts. To achieve this a Conservative government would create an independent Office for Budget Responsibility (OBR). The OBR would, as explained in the policy paper discussed above, produce 'fiscal forecasts at least once a year in advance of the Budget'. Along with these forecasts the OBR would 'make a forward-looking judgement of the sustainability of the public finances'. Crucially, this judgement would be made with reference to a very specific mandate to ensure that by the end of the forecast horizon, set by the Chancellor, net debt is falling as a percentage of GDP and that there is a balanced budget. Moreover, in making its judgement as to whether the public finances are sustainable in terms of the mandate, the OBR would have the power to state 'how much loosening or tightening of the fiscal policy [it estimates] would be necessary by the end of a given forecast horizon to meet the mandate'. However, the OBR would be precluded from suggesting what mix of loosening or tightening between tax revenues and spending it thinks should be employed (that is ultimately a political decision).

To ensure that the OBR's independent forecasts and judgements exert the necessary influence on the government of the day, the Conservatives would require the Chancellor to 'explain their reasoning to Parliament if they do not agree with the OBR's judgement of the public finances over the forecast horizon'. It's high time that the destabilising influence of politically motivated Treasury forecasts are brought to heel. A Conservative government would ensure that they are, and would as a result deliver a far better guarantee of fiscal responsibility than mere 'fiscal rules' could ever hope to achieve.

And the lessons from abroad support the case for an OBR. When Belgium and Netherlands used independent fiscal councils, their levels of debt fell radically immediately thereafter.

Ensuring sound financial regulation

The collapse of Britain's financial sector was an overwhelming demonstration of the failure of Labour's tripartite regulatory system. As John McFall, the Labour chairman of the Treasury Select Committee, said in 2007: '[The tripartite system] may be a Rolls-Royce when it sits on the shelf, it turns into an old banger when it gets on the ground.' Similarly, Professor Geoffrey Wood, in evidence to the House of Lords Select Committee on Economic Affairs, said: 'On occasions [the tripartite system] functioned with jaw-dropping incompetence . . . It was astonishing how badly their system worked . . . it is clear that nobody was actually in charge.' But the failure of the system didn't just result from nobody being in charge. There wasn't even anybody charged with putting the different pieces together to create a big picture.

However you cut it, the tripartite system has been weighed, measured, and found severely wanting. Accordingly, the Conservative Party has pledged to do away with it, abolishing the FSA and enhancing the regulatory power of the Bank of England. The case for this is quite clear: by vesting regulatory power in one institution you ensure that there is no uncertainty over who is in charge and no gaps in regulatory coverage.

What's more, the Conservatives would ensure that the newly empowered Bank of England had teeth. For example, the Bank would have the power to 'ensure that capital liquidity requirements recognise the additional risk implied by an institution's size and complexity', to impose much higher capital requirements on high-risk activities, and to further use capital requirements as a form of tax on 'risky bonus structures'.

Tax and spend

When Gordon Brown addressed the Labour Party conference in 1997 he signalled a fundamental shift in party thinking: 'We have learned from past mistakes . . . you cannot spend your way out of recession.' Yet just over ten years later we find that Brown as Prime Minister has tried desperately to do exactly that. Instead of leading the G20 out of recession as he promised, we were the last to leave. And thanks to all that spending, and more importantly all that borrowing, both before and during the recession, we find ourselves in an unprecedented position, as David Cameron made clear in November 2009:

Our national debt has doubled in the last five years . . . This year we are predicted to borrow almost 14 per cent of our GDP. That's nearly twice as much as when we nearly went bankrupt in the 1970s And the latest monthly figures show that public borrowing is eighty-eight times what it was in the same month last year.

Astonishingly, one pound in every four the government spends goes towards paying off the national debt. As Phillip Hammond, shadow Chief Secretary to the Treasury, pointed out in October 2009: 'By 2013 we will be spending £63 billion a year on interest on the national debt. Twice what we spend on schools. More than we spend on defence and transport put together.'

The deficit must be cut. On this matter all parties are agreed. But whilst Labour have engaged in internal battles on how honest to be with the public about the action needed to deal with it, the Conservative Party has been unflinchingly candid from the start. Under a Conservative government, action to cut the deficit would comprise two things: tax rises and public spending restraint.

The Conservatives have been equally candid about the balance to be struck between those two measures. As Hammond stated in the same 2009 speech: 'In our judgement, we are at the point where further significant tax increases will seriously erode Britain's competitiveness. So we concluded months ago that public spending would have to bear the brunt of the burden.'

Tax

Not only is the Conservative Party a low-tax party, but we recognise that in the current economy, with individuals, families and businesses struggling to make ends meet, now is not the time to take their hard-earned money out of their pockets.

In order to support businesses at this time, the Conservative Party would cut the small companies rate of corporation tax from 22p to 20p, and the main rate of corporation tax from 28p to 25p. These cuts would be paid for by scrapping complex reliefs and allowances. On top of this, as David Cameron has described, the Conservatives would 'abolish all tax on the first ten jobs new businesses create during the first two years of a Conservative government'. With the economy in its present state, it is more important than ever to ensure that everything possible is done to help businesses, established and new, to survive and prosper.

Moving to personal taxation, a Conservative government would ensure that marriage and civil partnerships are finally recognised in the UK's tax system (for more on this see the Family chapter). The Conservatives have additionally pledged to help first-time buyers by abolishing stamp duty on properties worth up to £250,000. This would equate to taking nine out of ten-first time buyers out of stamp duty altogether. Council tax is another area where we would ease the burden placed on hard-working individuals and families. A Conservative government would freeze council tax for two years and would pay for this by cutting spending on consultants and advertising. Furthermore, the Conservative Party has pledged to raise the inheritance tax threshold to £1 million, ensuring that for the vast majority of people the family home is taken out of inherit-ance tax once and for all. In order to pay for this, a Conservative government would place a flat-rate levy on all non-doms.

But some new taxes are inevitable. For example, the Conserva-tive Party has been very clear that it would introduce a range of new 'green taxes'. Whereas Labour have utilised green taxes as a stealth tax – using them to do little other than raise additional money for the Treasury – the Conservatives have made an unequivocal promise: any new green taxes that are primarily designed to change behaviour will be 'replacement taxes'. Any revenue from these taxes would be placed in a 'Families Fund', which would be used to reduce existing taxes on families. So whilst green taxes would go up, other taxes would go down to compensate, ensuring that families have no less money in their pockets.

One tax that any government would find difficult to avoid raising is VAT. At the moment it sits at 17.5 per cent, having come back to its usual level following an ill-conceived reduction to 15 per cent (which added £1 billion a month to the UK's debt). Although no policy has yet been set, it is quite likely that a Conservative government would have to increase VAT to 20 per cent, at least for a short period of time. But whereas Labour are all too eager to raise taxes and invent new ones wherever possible, a Conservative government would only raise taxes where it is absolutely necessary and utterly unavoidable.

Making tax simpler

The UK tax code is the longest in the world. At over 10,000 pages its nearest rival, the Indian tax code, is a full 1,000 pages shorter. Unsurprisingly, the code's complexity matches its length. And that's bad for business. If Britain is to regain its global economic competitiveness tax has to be made simpler. To achieve this, a Conservative government would create an Office of Tax Simplification (OTS). *Reconstruction* explains:

> The OTS will include HMRC and Treasury officials, academics and crucially members of the tax professions, whose remit will be to systematically examine the existing tax code and make proposals for simplification. It will become an authoritative independent and permanent voice on tax law . . . which will create a sustained and powerful institutional pressure for the simplification of the tax system.

Spending

Public spending has to be cut. As the independent Institute for Fiscal Studies made all too clear in its study of the 2009 Budget and Red Book, the necessity of public spending cuts transcends party political divides. According to the institute, if the deficit is to be dealt with, the next government will have to cut spending by 7 per cent across the board. What's more, the Institute points out, if the NHS is ring-fenced as the Conservatives have pledged, those cuts would increase to at least 10 per cent.

Only one party has been unhesitatingly honest from the very beginning about the need for cuts in public sector spending to deal with the deficit: the Conservative Party. Labour chose at first to deny that cuts were need, but when a leaked document made clear that Labour were considering cuts of up to 10 per cent the party began to change its tune. They then made the argument that cuts could be put off, as if the deficit were like a 'buy now, pay next year' sofa from DFS. And then, after the failed coup against Gordon Brown in January 2010, Alistair Darling announced that the next Public Spending Review will be 'the toughest we have had in twenty years'. Conveniently, though, Labour decided to postpone that review until after the election.

But public spending cuts don't have to mean a reduction in service delivery; indeed the Conservatives are committed to ensuring that the public sector starts to deliver more for less. There are three broad strands to the Conservative approach to cuts:

1. Spending cuts in the traditional sense;
2. Savings achieved through improved public sector productivity;
3. Savings achieved by addressing the root causes of problems that ultimately place demands on the public purse.

Spending cuts

The Conservative position on cuts is utterly clear, as David Cameron explained in his 'Age of Austerity' speech: 'The days of easy money are over, and we have no option but to weed out spending that is not essential.'

A Conservative government would scrap Labour's ID cards scheme. Not only would ID cards fail to protect us from terror attacks, fail to prevent illegal immigration and fail to prevent human traffic, they would also cost £20 billion to implement, according to the London School of Economics.

Along with this, the Conservatives would scrap the Contact-Point database, which holds data on all children under the age of eighteen in England. ContactPoint cost £41 million to run each year and creates an enormous risk to vulnerable children (which might explain why MPs' children aren't listed on it).

One body that absolutely can't avoid cuts is Parliament itself. Parliament is bloated and inefficient. For one thing, there are simply too many MPs. A Conservative government would cut the number of MPs by 10 per cent and close Parliament's unaffordable pension scheme to new members.

The regional assemblies in England would also face the axe, along with their associated bureaucratic costs. People rightly expect transparency and accountability from their government, and it's simply wrong for these unelected regional bodies to sit in judgement over the decisions of elected councillors.

And just as workers in the private sector are feeling the pinch of pay cuts and pay freezes, so too should workers in the public sector, and that starts with government ministers. A Conservative government would cut the ministers' pay by 5 per cent and freeze it at that level for the full term of parliament. As for the wider public sector, a pay freeze is inevitable regardless of who's in government. That being so, the Conservatives would institute a one-year public sector pay freeze in 2011. Crucially, though, this freeze won't affect those earning less than £18,000 per year. Soldiers serving in Afghanistan would also be excused from this freeze. As David Cameron has said, they're risking their lives and 'we owe them so much more'.

For those who earn the most in the public sector, the message is clear: the Conservatives would demand a great deal more (see further below). Crucially, the absurd situation where individuals on the public purse often earn more than the Prime Minister must be dealt with. As George Osborne set out: 'Anyone who wishes to pay a public servant more than the Prime Minister will have to put it before the Chancellor. I am not expecting a long queue.'

Cutting the cost of quangos

The proliferation of quangos under Labour could be likened to the spread of wildfire. David Cameron highlighted the problem in July 2009: 'The problem today is that too much of what government does is actually done by people that no one can vote out, by organisations that feel no pressure to answer for what happens and in a way that is relatively unaccountable.'

And quangos don't come cheap. The real cost is difficult to ascertain, but it falls somewhere between the official figure of £34 billion and £64 billion (and the number of quangos sits likewise between 790 and 1,100). And there are sixty-eight quango heads who earn more than the Prime Minister.

A Conservative government would bring the cost of quangos down significantly. For a start they would have their communications departments stripped away and would be reduced to an administrative rather than political role, lowering the visibility and cost of their chief executives. But more fundamentally, the Conservatives start from the presumption that wherever possible ministers should carry out their duties through their departments. This isn't to say the Conservatives are anti-quango. Rather, they recognise that quangos have an important role to play, but that it is confined within a specific set of parameters. The test which the Conservatives would employ for whether a quango is needed is simple: if the execution of a particular policy should not be subject to political influence then it should be kept at arm's length (i.e. through a quango). Any quangos that do not meet this test would be abolished and their duties returned to the relevant minister and department.

Improving productivity

Public spending cuts don't have to mean cuts in public service delivery. Public spending was £396 billion in 1997, £720 billion in 2009. But this increase has not been matched by a commensurate rise in productivity. Indeed, according to the Office of National Statistics, quality-adjusted public sector productivity actually decreased, by 3.4 per cent. Despite almost doubling spending, the public sector became less productive! And yet during that same period productivity in the private sector rose by over 30 per cent. As Philip Hammond explained in 2009, if the public sector had achieved the same productivity gains as the private sector it would have saved the taxpayer £60 billion a year. The lesson from this is clear and simple; public sector spending cuts don't have to affect service delivery. The public sector simply has to deliver more for less. David Cameron says:

> Only in government do people automatically think that the way to get things done is to spend more money. But it's not true . . . On my watch it will be simple: if you do more for less you get promoted, if you do less for more you get sacked.

As a starting point, a Conservative government would place a contractual obligation on senior civil servants to save the taxpayer money. Philip Hammond describes how this would take effect:

> The principal job of the Chief Secretary [of the Treasury] in the next government will be to ensure that the machinery in the engine room of government is calibrated to deliver a continuous stream of productivity improvements, enhancing the efficiency of public services, delivering improvements in outcomes, even as budgets are reduced.

But placing the burden of efficiency on the shoulders of permanent secretaries alone would not ensure that productivity in the public sector meets that of the private sector. To ensure that already identified efficiency savings are implemented across the public sector when a Conservative government takes office and to imbue our public sector with a culture in which, as Hammond puts it, 'the pursuit of efficiency becomes self-sustaining', the Conservatives would create a Public Services Productivity Advisory Board. This board would comprise 'prominent individuals with experience and understanding' of the productivity agenda. Working with a new Conservative government, it would ensure that the efficiency drives of the past are turned into 'an institutionalised culture change in the public sector of the future'.

Perhaps the most innovative approach to ensuring that the public sector does more with less is the Conservative Party's plan to, as Hammond has explained, 'transfer the ownership of central government property into a publicly owned, professionally managed, asset company, which will charge departments rent for their use.' By taking this one simple step an wonderful incentive would be created for government departments to use central government property worth billions of pounds more efficiently. Hammond points out: 'If they reduce what they use, they will make cash savings.'

To further ingrain the importance of delivering more for less, a Conservative government would roll out payment by results. Naturally implementation would differ from department to department, but, as Hammond summarises, the end result is the same: 'If you don't deliver, you don't get paid.'

A final point that can't pass without mention is the Conservative commitment to transparency. It's not enough that people are contractually obliged to save, or that the government promises to work hard to deliver more for less. The only way to guarantee that savings are made is by ensuring transparency. Accordingly, under a Conservative government members of the public could look up every item of public spending over £25,000, and would have access to the names of everyone in the public sector who earns over £150,000 a year.

Getting to the root of the problem

In the longer term, the Conservative Party aims to fundamentally reduce the demands on the state by lessening the need for state intervention in people's lives. That means reducing crime, long-term unemployment and welfare dependency, drug addiction, educational failure – the list goes on. To achieve this, the Conservatives have committed to addressing the root causes of many of these problems (for an example of how this approach would work, see the Family chapter). By taking this approach, the long-term effects are clear: a reduced role for the state and a less costly state as a result.

Getting people into work

At the time of writing there are 2.5 million people unemployed (moreover, the government projects that unemployment will not reach pre-recession levels for at least another ten years). Roughly 2,000 people lose their jobs every day, 2.6 million are on incapacity benefits, there are 3.3 million homes in which no adult works (17 per cent of all households), and we have the highest level of youth unemployment in the EU. And tempting though it might be to point to the recession when explaining the fact that so many are not in employment, it must be borne in mind that even before the recession began there were, as declared by the Department of Work and

Pensions, just under five million people already out of work and on benefits. When it comes to unemployment, Britain is in crisis.

Labour's response has been pathetic. Since 1997 Labour have launched more than twenty national employment programmes such as New Deal, Flexible New Deal, New Deal for Musicians and Workstep. But for all this effort and expense, the results have been lacklustre. For example, according to the DWP's own figures, New Deal 25 Plus (one of the many New Deal variants) managed to get fewer than one in four of the people it dealt with into employment. And as the Conservative Party highlights in its *Get Britain Working* policy paper: 'Multiple evaluations have concluded that the number of people who have entered the world of work thanks to the job-seekers allowance regime and New Deals, as opposed to those who would have found work anyway, is very low.' And incredibly, Labour have yet to create any mandatory programmes to assist individuals on incapacity benefit into work. For all Labour's frantic activity, little has been achieved. It's perhaps no surprise then that there's yet to be a Labour government that leaves office with unemployment lower than when it came in.

A practical plan for reform

In order to succeed where Labour have failed, a Conservative government would do away with Labour's vast array of back-to-work programmes, which categorise people by the type of benefit they claim, and would instead introduce, as described in *Get Britain Working*, a 'single, fully funded integrated programme' called The Work Programme (TWP). All individuals of working age who are currently unemployed and claiming benefits (including incapacity benefit) would be referred to TWP. And because some individuals require more help than others to find work, people would be moved onto TWP at varying rates. For example, someone who hadn't worked in years would be moved onto the programme very quickly, whereas someone with a strong employment history could be referred up to twelve months after first making a benefits claim.

But perhaps the most important aspect of TWP is that it would be delivered by private and voluntary organisations, and those organisations would be paid purely on the basis of the results they achieve. There are two strands to this. First, whereas, for example, Labour's Flexible New Deal pays providers a fixed fee for each claimant they deal with – and in so doing creates an incentive for providers to put less effort into those individuals who require more help – TWP would employ a system of varying fees for claimants. So, for example, a claimant who has been out of work for many years and has very few skills would be worth more than a highly skilled claimant. Secondly, providers under TWP would only be paid for a client when they got them into long-term employment. So whereas, to use the Flexible New Deal example again, Labour awards providers 70 per cent of their fee once a claimant has been in work for a mere thirteen weeks, TWP would take a much longer-term approach, ensuring that providers take a similar approach when helping claimants into work.

Crucially, because a Conservative government would pay by results, they would ensure that providers have the freedom to innovate in achieving those results, for example by developing their own training or mentoring programmes. But to support providers in their efforts to get claimants into work, a Conservative government would also create a range of additional programmes within the TWP framework. One such example is Youth Action for Work.

Youth Action for Work

As indicated above, the UK has the highest rate of youth unemployment in the EU. In order to address this problem, the Conservative Party has committed to tackling one of the biggest challenges many of Britain's young unemployed face when seeking work: a lack of skills and experience. The Youth Action for Work (YAW) programme would be available to any young person who has been on jobseeker's allowance for six months. It could be used by TWP providers for such claimants when they felt it was appropriate).

Many of the opportunities that would be provided under YAW will be discussed in more detail in the Universities and Higher Education chapter. They include creating 100,000 new apprenticeships and fully funding the 77,000 existing ones that Labour have only part funded, providing an extra 50,000 places at further education colleges and creating an extra 10,000 university places in the first year of a Conservative government. However, YAW would also include a range of opportunities on top of those already discussed. A prime example of this is the Work Pairing scheme, through which a Conservative government would deliver 100,000 six-month work experience placements with sole traders for 16–19-year-olds (with an emphasis placed on those with little existing work experience). The Conservative Party understands the barriers that many of Britain's young people face in the employment market; YAW is a first step in helping them overcome those barriers.

Working for welfare

Unlike Labour, a Conservative government wouldn't allow people to claim jobseeker's allowance indefinitely. As *Get Britain Working* makes clear, 'anyone who has been through the new system without finding work and has claimed jobseeker's allowance for longer than two of the previous three years would be required to join a mandatory long-term community work scheme as a condition of continuing to receive benefit support'. It is only right that the generosity of the taxpayer be respected, and this simple measure would ensure that it is.

Supporting business

Clearly, any strategy to reduce unemployment must take also

account of the needs of employers. For some examples of this, see the Tax and Spend and Localism chapters.

Paying for it

There's no doubt that the Conservative Party's plans for getting people into work are bold. But as ever, commitments by politicians don't mean anything if they can't be paid for. However, as the above would be financed by reallocating funding for Labour's existing programmes, the only additional cost would be an upfront one over three years of £600 million. To pay for this a Conservative government would retest all those who currently receive incapacity benefit, and those who are found to be fit for work would be moved over to the less costly jobseeker's allowance. Indeed, it is a scandal that this has not been done already.

Localism

The common thread that stands out across the range of policy areas discussed in this book is the Conservatives' fundamental and unshakeable commitment to decentralising responsibility and power. As the party's *Control Shift* policy paper states:

Conservatives want to build a stronger, safer society where opportunity and power are spread much more widely and fairly. We believe communities are strongest when everyone has a free and fair say in the decisions that affect them. From local council services and planning

decisions to local policing priorities, people should have as much
power and choice as possible . . . Without real local democracy, communities are made weaker: social responsibility, civic involvement and
the inclusion of vulnerable people in social life are all being inhibited.

Under Labour the distrust for local decision-making has been
all too apparent. And it is here that perhaps the greatest distinc-
tion between the Conservative and Labour parties can be found.
Whereas Labour remain their commitment to accumulation and
execution of power at the centre, the Conservatives are committed
to ensuring that when any decision is taken, it is taken as closely to
the people affected by it as possible.

Examples of this fundamental difference in approach are found
throughout this book, and for that reason this chapter will confine
itself to simply providing a brief overview of how this difference in
approach will appear across a range of areas. Under a Conservative
government a radical agenda of localism would be realised in two
main ways:

1. Pushing power downwards and outwards;
2. Putting more information in the hands of the people.

Pushing power down and out

The role of local government is a prime example of how the Conservatives would radically shift power away from the centre. For
example, as discussed further in the Countryside chapter, whereas
Labour have dictated from the centre how many new houses must
be built by specific local authorities, a Conservative government
would put local councils in control by giving them an absolute
say on how many houses they would build and where they would
build them. The Conservatives would also empower local councils
to support local businesses by allowing them to levy business rate
discounts, and would allow local businesses to block business rate

hikes where they were too harsh. Crucially, whereas local councils may currently take action only where they are specifically authorised to do so by statute, the Conservatives would introduce new powers giving them the freedom to take action where it is in the interest of local residents, even if there isn't explicit authority in legislation. Councils would only be held back in those instances where their authority is specifically limited by law. And when it comes to council tax (which has doubled under Labour), local councils would have to hold a referendum if they wanted to increase it above the national threshold. Equally, whereas under Labour only councils have the power to deliver local referendums, the Conservatives would give residents the power to force a local referendum where they can obtain the signatures of 5 per cent of local citizens. Furthermore, a Conservative government would provide a referendum in the twelve largest cities in England on whether they want an elected mayor with executive powers. The Conservative Party would place power and accountability back in the hands of local councils and in so doing make them more answerable to local people.

Moving away from local government per se, the Conservatives would also deliver radical change in policing. As discussed in the Crime chapter, a Conservative government would make police forces accountable to the communities they serve rather than the Home Secretary by creating locally elected police commissioners. If local people aren't happy with policing, they'll have someone they can call to account.

Similarly, as discussed in the Schools chapter, in education a Conservative government would empower parents, and others, to set up new schools when they aren't happy with existing ones. These new Academy schools would be completely independent of the local authority and financed by putting parents in charge of the taxpayer money allocated to their child's education each year.

The examples are many and varied, but the central premise is the same throughout; the Conservative Party believes passionately in placing decision-making power as close to the people affected as possible.

Opening up information

It goes without saying that in order for people to exercise their new-found power effectively, they need to have as much information as possible. Using one of the above examples, what point would there be in creating elected police commissioners if people didn't have access to detailed information about local crime rates?

The Conservative Party recognises this. As explained in the Crime chapter, the Conservatives would require police forces to publish a monthly map detailing, street by street, how much crime and what types of crime are occurring, ensuring the public are well informed and equipped to hold the police to account.

This kind of comprehensive information-sharing is central to the Conservative Party's localist agenda, and further instances can be found throughout this book. As the examples above demonstrate, the Conservatives understand that local decisions make for better decisions.

Schools

Good education is the cornerstone of any successful society – equipping the next generation for the challenges they will face and ensuring the growth of opportunity so that a person's ability to succeed in life is determined not by their parents' wealth but by their own talent.

When it came to power, the Labour Party promised a bright future. Tony Blair proudly proclaimed his commitment to 'education, education, education'. But here as in so many areas, the British people have been let down by the Labour government. For whilst we're told that education in schools is tremendously successful, the raw data proves otherwise. Michael Gove MP, shadow Secretary of State for Children Schools and Families, made this clear in a November 2009 speech:

> The sad truth about our schools today is that, far from making opportunity more equal, they only deepen the divide between the rich and poor, the fortunate and the forgotten. It is a profoundly dispiriting story. The poorest students in our schools are those pupils eligible for free school meals [FSM]. From the beginning to the end of primary school, the achievement gap between FSM and non-FSM children widens – and from eleven to fourteen the gap widens further still. Examine the picture of achievement at GCSE and the landscape only looks bleaker. Employers are disinclined to take any GCSE seriously unless the candidate secures at least a C pass. Of the 75,000 children on free school meals each year, almost half do not get a single C grade in any GCSE.

As Gove goes on to point out, in schools where more than half the pupils are entitled to FSM a mere 13 per cent meet the benchmark standard of five GCSE passes. In 'hard' subjects such as science, the figures are utterly depressing: more children eligible for FSM take media studies at GCSE than the three sciences combined. And at A-level the tragic story only continues: out of the 20,000 children who achieved three A grades, only 189 were amongst those eligible for FSM. And almost 40 per cent of 11-year-old primary school pupils fail to meet the government's basic level in reading, writing and maths every year. Radical action is desperately needed to improve Britain's schools.

But whereas Labour only offer more of the same, the Conservative Party offers a fundamentally different approach.

Discipline

It goes without saying that good schools have good discipline. But under Labour, teachers have found that the balance of power has shifted away from them and in favour of pupils. The clearest illustration of this is the pathetic state of a school's ultimate sanction for unruly behaviour, expulsion. These days, when a headteacher orders the expulsion of a pupil, that decision can be overturned by an appeals panel – with no connection to the school and no direct understanding of its circumstances – run by the local authority. Alarmingly, as the *Raising the Bar* policy paper highlights, 'one in four appeals is won by the appellant and half these children return to their original school'. What's more, schools which expel students have financial penalties imposed on them. As a result of this, headteachers have become reluctant to expel the most disruptive students and are opting instead, often on multiple occasions in a single school year, to suspend them for periods of time. The net result is that the headteacher's authority is utterly undermined and disruptive pupils are only encouraged in their behaviour.

Under the Conservatives the balance of power would shift back to teachers. Returning to expulsion, for example, the Conservatives would end the right of appeal to local authority panels and would instead allow an appeal only to the governors of the school in question. On top of that the Conservatives would end schools' financial penalties imposed on schools for expulsions. Crucially, though, the Conservatives are not blind to the plight of children who are expelled and find themselves in pupil referral units (PRUs), a system which Ofsted has described as 'the least successful of all in ensuring good progress of the pupils who attended'. A Conservative government would bring serious reform to PRUs, ensuring that, as *Raising the Bar* puts it, they 'adopt the best practice of those units that are graded by Ofsted as Outstanding'.

The empowerment of headteachers doesn't end with expulsion. For example, a Conservative government would give them the power, in Gove's words, 'to ban, search for, and confiscate any items they think may cause violence or disruption'. Incredibly, Labour are opposed to this measure on human rights grounds. On top of this, new legislation would be introduced to give teachers the right to ban disruptive devices, such as mobile phones, from the classroom. And the legal requirement for twenty-four hours' notice of detentions would be abolished.

Finally, one of the biggest challenges for teachers on the front line is removing violent and disruptive children from the classroom; the threat of legal action on the part of those children is all too real. The Conservatives would therefore replace the existing Use of Force Guidance and make it easier for teachers to take action when needed without having to worry about a potential backlash.

A Conservative government would ensure that teachers have the power they need to deal with disruptive behaviour and ensure that it doesn't go on to have a negative impact on the vast majority of children who simply want to learn.

Recruiting the best

A common theme of those countries whose education systems lead the world – such as Finland, South Korea and Singapore – is the selectiveness of their teacher recruitment programmes. For example, only the top 10 per cent of university graduates in Finland are eligible to apply to become teachers. A Conservative government would, to paraphrase Michael Gove, follow this path. Firstly, individuals wanting to become primary school teachers would have to have achieved at least a B grade in both English and maths at GCSE rather than the current requirement of a C grade in either English or maths. Gove explains: 'This means that primary teachers will come from the top third of students rather than the top two-thirds as now.' And when it comes to those who want to obtain a PGCE in order to become secondary school teachers, the Conservatives have made clear that the taxpayer would only fund individuals who have obtained a 2:2 or higher in their undergraduate degrees. As Gove made clear in the same speech: 'Deep subject knowledge is a prerequisite for success in secondary school teaching.'

It would be foolish, though, to hope that raising the barrier to entry would by itself provide the necessary incentive to convince to very best to enter teaching. Money talks. And with that in mind the Conservatives would devolve much more power to headteachers with respect to remuneration. When a teacher performs better than their peers they should be paid better.

Of course, getting the best teachers isn't just about recruiting the best; it's also about weeding out the weakest. With that in mind the Conservatives have committed to a radical change in the compulsory literacy and numeracy tests which teachers sit. Rather than allowing teachers an infinite number of resits, as is currently the case, the Conservatives would permit just one. If you don't make the cut, you get cut. Britain's children deserve no less.

Getting to the root of the problem: improving literacy

As highlighted above, almost 40 per cent of eleven-year-old primary school pupils fail to meet the government's basic level in reading. *Raising the Bar* explains: 'The knock-on effect of failing to master the basics has a severe impact on achievement at secondary school: only fourteen per cent of those not reaching Level 4 by age eleven achieve five good GCSEs five years later.' Clearly, a large measure of dealing with educational failure comes down to improving how children are taught to read. To achieve this, a Conservative government would encourage a return to synthetic phonics rather than today's more popular sight vocabulary approach to teaching reading, as the Conservatives highlighted in *Raising the Bar*.

> Evidence has shown that children whose teaching is based on sight vocabulary have a one in four chance of failing, with boys much more likely to fail than girls. With phonics less than one in twenty have this risk, and boys do as well as girls. Synthetic phonics can help combat the difficulties faced by poorer pupils who do not grow up in a book-rich environment.

Empowering through choice

A corollary of the poor state of education in Britain's schools is that there are far too few good places. Too many children are consigned to educational failure by virtue of little more than their parent's lack of options when it comes to good schools. As Michael Gove described in his November 2009 speech: 'About 100,000 parents a year do not get their first choice of school. Many others in some parts of the country do not have a "preference" amongst local schools because they consider them all bad.'

This has to change; parents desperately need real choice for their children's education. And real choice means ensuring the availability of many more good school places. The Conservative response to this challenge is two-fold:

1. A recognition that independent schools perform better;
2. Removing the state's monopoly on the power to set up new schools.

The Conservative Party's recognition that independent schools perform better is not a reference to fee-paying independent schools.

Rather, when the Conservatives talk about 'independent schools' what they mean is the academy style of schools, which are free to all and independent from local authorities. In that same speech, Gove drew attention to a number of academies, including:

- Mossbourne City Academy in Hackney – 85 per cent of its pupils achieved good GCSEs including English and maths
- Thomas Telford School in Telford – 99.4 per cent of its pupils achieved at least ten good GCSEs including English and maths

Gove remarked: 'Their success now is powerful, incontestable proof that it is not intake which makes a school outstanding but independence; it is not conformity with bureaucratic diktats which drives success but accountability to parents.'

The Conservative Party has not been shy in acknowledging the huge success which the Labour-pioneered academies have had. But whereas internal opposition has prevented Labour from taking the academy idea to its logical conclusion and thereby realising its true potential, the Conservative Party has no such limitations. The Conservatives would ensure that the number of independent academies grew rapidly.

Firstly, the Conservatives would allow any existing school to apply to become an academy. And those schools which have been rated 'good' or 'outstanding' would automatically be approved for academy status; enabling over 400 secondary schools to become new Thomas Telfords and Mossbournes within a matter of weeks after a Conservative government came into office. Crucially, the Conservatives would, as Gove puts it, 'extend the Academy programme to primary schools, allowing them to innovate and flourish'.

But turning existing schools into new academies is only part of the solution. As indicated above, the Conservative Party is committed to breaking the state monopoly on creating new schools. So whilst existing schools would be allowed to apply to become academies, the Conservatives would also, in Gove's words, 'make it much easier for educational charities, groups of parents and teachers, cooperatives and others to start new academies.' So if parents aren't happy with the schools in their area they can start their own.

To pay for the capital cost of these new schools a Conservative government would create a new fund comprising money reallocated from the overly bureaucratic Building Schools for the Future programme. All told, by reallocating only 15 per cent of the programme's future funding the new academies fund would receive £4.5 billion over nine years. This would provide the capital necessary to create at least 220,000 new school places.

As for the running costs for these new academies, Gove explains that they would simply 'receive the same government funding as other schools in their community for every pupil they teach'. On top of that, though, parents would effectively become masters of the money which the government spends on every child. 'Parents will have the power to take their child out of a state school, apply to a new academy, and automatically transfer the per-pupil funding from the old school to the new academy.' And to encourage the creation of academies in more deprived areas, the Conservatives have committed to providing additional capital on top of the annual per-pupil funding for children in these areas.

Universities, skills and vocational training

At the university level there is need for serious reform if we are to equip the next generation with the knowledge they will need to compete and succeed in the 21st-century marketplace. And as far as skills and vocational training are concerned, it has become tragically clear that the Labour government has failed Britain's young people in almost every way.

Universities

Despite the value of a university education, young people with aspirations to attend university have been resolutely let down by Labour. Despite their commitment to getting 50 per cent of young people into university, the proportion of young people going to university has barely changed in over eight years. What's more, when the numbers of young people wanting to go to university increased sharply in 2009, universities found themselves being fined for taking on extra students.

Rather than punishing universities for responding to demand, the Conservatives would provide an extra 10,000 places in their first year of government, ensuring that students who meet the grade are not turned away. Naturally, this would come at a cost: £300 million. But rather than taking Labour's approach and simply borrowing to meet expenditure, the Conservatives have come up with an innovative solution, one which benefits graduates and new students alike.

Presently, there is no incentive to pay off a student loan early. The Conservatives would change that: graduates would be given a

10 per cent discount for any early repayments over £500, including up-front repayment. Such an incentive would yield additional short-term income. And based on projections from a similar scheme in New Zealand, the Conservative Party's incentive system would generate at least £300 million over a three-year period, all of which would then be recycled back into universities in order to pay for the additional 10,000 places.

Furthermore, it is clear that for those with vocational quali-fications rather than more traditional A-levels, the transition to university is often far from straightforward. Despite the inherent value of vocational qualifications, the impression often given, implic-itly or explicitly, is that they don't cut the mustard like their more academic counterparts. This simply isn't true, and a Conservative government would see that action is taken to address this problem.

Skills/vocational training

Skills and vocational training in the UK are, frankly, in a terrible state. There are almost one million young people not in educa-tion, employment or training (NEETs) and, despite all Labour's grandstanding, the number of people in apprenticeships has fallen by a third. Bold plans are needed if this terrible situation is to be reversed. When it comes to delivering the revolution needed, a Conservative government would reallocate existing government spending to focus on three areas: apprenticeships, community learn-ing and careers advice.

The Conservatives would create 100,000 new apprenticeships and fully fund the 77,000 apprenticeships that are currently only partially funded, through an investment of £775 million. Bearing in mind that currently only 10 per cent of employers provide appren-ticeships and that the vast majority of those are large businesses, a £2,000 'bonus' would be paid to small and medium-sized businesses for each apprentice they took on board, helping them cover the costs associated with taking on and training these individuals. By taking this two-pronged approach, young people would benefit and, over time, so would small and medium-sized businesses.

Separately, the Conservative Party's commitment to community learning is a reflection of one of its most fundamental beliefs, namely, that strong communities help build a strong society. There are two central strands to the approach a Conservative government would take in this area:

1. Adult and community learning;
2. Getting NEETs back on track.

As we point out in *Building Skills, Transforming Lives*:

> Funding for adult and community learning has been cut under Labour, despite the fact that it offers an important, locally based route to training for many people who have been out of the labour market, such as parents or carers wanting to re-enter paid work or people needing to update their skills after redundancy . . . Adult social learning has immense social value that we are keen to recognise more fully.

This form of adult learning would take place at further education colleges and the range of subjects covered would naturally be very broad. But by way of example, one challenge that often affects adults who want to re-enter the work force, particularly in a completely new field, is a lack of modern workplace skills such as basic IT. Adult community learning ensures that just this kind of information and knowledge is available to people in the form of flexible short courses right in the heart of their communities. A Conservative government would ensure that adult community learning finally receives the funding it has sorely lacked under Labour by creating a £100 million Community Learning Fund to enable further education colleges to provide exactly these kinds of course.

When it comes to NEETs the Conservative Party understands that for these young people the experience of formal education in school was not one they enjoyed. For these young people the path back into education often appears utterly unappealing. But that doesn't mean we should simply give up on them. As the above policy paper makes clear:

> Small steps back into education, rather than substantial courses leading to full qualifications, can offer a less challenging prospect for someone who has not got on with the school system first time around. Short courses that enhance a young person's confidence and basic employability can be delivered through locally based training providers, including further education colleges, as they are best placed to understand the particular needs of local economies and community groups.

To ensure that exactly this kind of targeted assistance and learning is delivered to young people who find themselves out of school, without qualifications, out of work and unable to take advantage of more formal education, the Conservatives would create a £100 million NEETs Fund. Only by investing in these young people can we get their lives back on track, and the Conservative Party is the only party with a clear vision for achieving this.

To complement such fundamental improvements in access to university, availability of apprenticeships and quality of community learning, a Conservative government would radically overhaul the provision of careers advice in the UK. After all, what good are skills and training if a person doesn't know where they're heading? Firstly, the Conservatives have committed to providing £180 million to pay for a 'careers adviser in every secondary school and college in the country'. And secondly, but no less importantly, they would provide £100 million to create 'a new all-age careers advice service which will provide a community-based source of advice and guidance for people of all ages'.

Finally, unlike Labour the Conservative Party won't make spending commitments without explaining how those commitments will be met. To cover the cost of the measures listed above the Conservatives have pledged to refocus failing programmes currently run by the Labour government in the areas mentioned. An example is the government's Train to Gain scheme, which has failed to meet its objective of 'providing support to hard-to-reach employers'. The Conservatives would refocus Train to Gain's budget of over £1 billion 'in order to pay employers directly for the provision of genuine apprenticeships that build the skills they need and to help adults not in work or training to skill up and re-enter the workforce'. All told, by refocusing various failing or underperforming programmes the Conservative Party has calculated that it would yield over £1.3 billion to cover the cost of its radical plans to improve skills and vocational training.

Health

One British institution soars above all others in terms of its place in the people's hearts: the NHS. Since 1948 it has provided reassurance that from 'cradle to grave', regardless of circumstance and determined purely on the basis of need, all who required medical treatment would receive it free of charge at the point of delivery. A universal service, universally loved.

It would be wrong to suggest that the Conservatives have always been perceived as a friend of the NHS. It is perhaps unsurprising therefore that one of the biggest obstacles in front of David Cameron's Conservative Party was convincing the public that not only had the party changed, but that it had become the party of the NHS.

That the Conservative Party has changed is beyond doubt, that they are the party of the NHS is unequivocally clear. But for those who have not yet been convinced by this, they should consider for a moment the person who leads the party. In his first speech as Conservative Party leader Cameron paid tribute to the NHS and all it had done and continued to do for his son Ivan, who had severe cerebral palsy and epilepsy: 'I believe that the creation of the NHS is one of the greatest achievements of the twentieth century. When your family relies on the NHS all the time – day after day, night after night – you really know just how precious it is.'

The commitment of David Cameron, and the commitment of the Conservative Party as a whole, to the NHS could not be stronger. And when that commitment is combined with the policy laid out below, it is clear that the Conservative Party is the only party that can deliver for the NHS.

Some startling facts

Despite the fact that NHS resources have more than doubled since 1997 the Office of National Statistics has shown that productivity in the NHS has decreased by 2.5 per cent year on year.

As the Conservative Party's *Renewal Plan for a Better NHS* points out, 'every year around 230,000 people in England are diagnosed with cancer. Only 45 per cent of cancer patients in England survive for five years after diagnosis.' By way of comparison, in Sweden the five-year survival rate is 60 per cent. Even if the NHS was to achieve the EU average for five-year cancer survival rates that would mean another 4,600 people being saved each year. Achieving Sweden's survival rate would mean an incredible 34,500 lives being saved. And it doesn't stop with cancer. Every year, as the same policy paper makes clear, '275,000 people in England have a heart attack . . . 11.8 per cent of people in the UK die within thirty days.' In New Zealand the proportion of people that die within thirty days is drastically lower, 5.4 per cent. If the UK were to achieve the EU average for survival another 4,400 lives would be saved. And if New Zealand's survival rate were achieved another 17,600 lives would be saved. The list goes on.

These aren't just abstract figures, they're living, breathing individuals. People with families, husbands, wives, mothers, fathers, brothers, sisters, sons, daughters. The NHS is a wonderful achievement, but it's all too clear that significant improvement is needed.

The Conservative Party has made it its mission to raise the standards of the NHS to the best in the EU. As Andrew Lansley, the shadow Health Secretary, said in his 2009 Conservative Party conference speech: 'If we could be as effective as other European countries we could save up to 100,000 extra lives a year.' Achieving this will be no easy task, but the Conservative Party has made clear the steps it would take in government to see this task accomplished.

Firstly, the Conservatives have committed to increase spending on the NHS in real terms, starting with the new Chancellor's first Budget. But it isn't just about more spending, it's about smart spending and ensuring that more of the NHS budget goes to the frontline. Lansley explained in the same 2009 speech:

We will cut the cost of health service central bureaucracy by a third during the next parliament. Primary care trusts. Strategic health authorities. The health quangos. And the Department of Health itself. They spend a total of £4.5 billion in administration every year. So we will cut that bill by £1.5 billion within four years. All this from the back office to the frontline. We will tolerate no waste. No inflation. No poor value for money in NHS budgets.

But increased levels of spending combined with a redistribution of funds in favour of the frontline aren't on their own going to transform the NHS into the most effective health service in the EU. Much more is required.

Outcomes, not process

Any changes made by the Conservative Party to the NHS would not be ideological; as the party makes clear in the *Renewal Plan for a Better NHS*, it is 'committed to providing [the NHS] with the funding it needs to deliver high standards of healthcare to all, free at the point of use, based on need, not ability to pay'. Instead, the changes would be procedural and structural. Nowhere is this clearer than in the party's approach to targets in the NHS.

In his time as Chancellor and Prime Minister, Gordon Brown imposed a total of 101 targets on the NHS. These targets have placed the emphasis on processes rather than outcomes. The most famous example is the four-hour waiting limit at A&E.

Of course, there's nothing wrong with aspiring to see waiting times reduced. But the emphasis on process, in this case achieving a waiting time of no more than four hours, had unexpected consequences. The BBC has reported a practice that has evolved whereby A&Es move patients into 'assessment units' before they have exceeded the four-hour time limit. These units are often mixed sex and require patients to wait on trolleys rather than beds. What's more, patients are often subjected to very long waits in these 'half-way houses' between A&E and hospital, whilst the A&E department is able to tell the government that it has met its waiting time target. John Heyworth, from the College of Emergency Medicine, said: 'We know these areas are being used frequently purely to admit patients to meet the target and quite often they are not properly equipped and staffed.'

The trade union Unison has also uncovered shocking practices designed to ensure that the four-hour target is met: particularly, keeping patients in ambulances outside A&E units so as prevent the waiting time clock from starting. Unison spokeswoman Mary Maguire described one especially shocking example: 'A sixteen-year-old terminally ill cancer patient died after waiting over an hour for an ambulance to transfer him. Three ambulances could have reached him but they were tied up waiting to hand over patients to A&E. It happens time and time again.' Unsurprisingly, the four-hour target doesn't just bring distorted clinical priorities, it also comes with a hefty price tag, as the *Renewal Plan* highlights: 'Over the last five years, £2 billion has been spent solely on pursuing the four-hour limit at A&E.' And that was two years ago.

Sadly, the four-hour target isn't an isolated example of the damaging effect Labour's targets have had. The Conservatives' *The Patient Will See You Now* policy paper highlights the plight of women who have undergone a mastectomy:

A mastectomy is often recommended for women diagnosed with breast cancer, followed by follow-up (or 'adjuvant') radiotherapy to kill off stray cancer cells. However, the government's target – of women with breast cancer receiving their first treatment within two months – does not apply to follow-up treatment. As a result, follow-up radiotherapy is left untargeted.

The result is hardly surprising:

In 1998, 39 per cent of patients received their adjuvant radiotherapy more than four weeks after their surgery (four weeks is the maximum acceptable waiting time for adjuvant radiotherapy, as defined by the Joint Collegiate for Oncology in 1993). By 2005, however, 53 per cent of patients were seen outside the maximum acceptable waiting time.

Such results are nothing short of a national scandal. In his 2009 party conference speech, David Cameron was explicit: 'With their targets and bureaucratic control, Labour have actually created a system that forces NHS staff to follow rules that can actively cause harm to the health of patients.' And for that reason the Conservatives would 'scrap all centrally imposed targets relating to clinical processes, and replace them with a new focus on outcomes'.

This radical change of emphasis would lead to a similarly radical change of results and approach. Frontline managers would be freed from conforming with specific practices to meet the process-based targets and would instead be able to embrace those processes and procedures that produce the best outcomes. Rather than focusing their efforts and resources on ensuring that the four-hour wait box is ticked (even if it means patients waiting much longer in reality), they would be incentivised towards focusing on the outcomes for the patients in A&E.

Central to the Conservative Party's strategy is the decision to make the results of NHS treatment along with the healthcare experiences of patients publicly available. As explained in the *Renewal Plan*, this would 'enable patients, NHS professionals and the general public to see, for example, which hospitals perform well for a particular kind of surgery, or if a local GP has a good record for delivering good outcomes for patients. Patients and healthcare commissioners will then be able to judge providers by their results and make their choices over where to go for care accordingly. With funding following patients, patient choice will drive powerful incentives for providers to raise standards of care.' For more on patient choice and funding following patients see below.

Critically, thanks to this radical shift in emphasis frontline NHS staff would no longer be accountable to bureaucrats and politicians in Whitehall and would instead be accountable to patients. Above all else this means drastically improved standards, as the Conservatives have explained:

Unlike with Labour's process-driven targets, under our system professionals within an autonomous NHS will be free to make the right clinical decisions they feel will help achieve the outcomes we want to see. Patients and healthcare commissioners will be able to judge providers against their success in meeting these targets and make their choices accordingly, while the funding regime will reward success and encourage underperforming providers to improve.

Power to patients: transforming the patient–GP relationship

The Conservative Party's plans for the NHS place the patient in control. As indicated above, this in part means that frontline staff would be shifted from being accountable to politicians and bureaucrats to being accountable to patients. But that's only a start. For the Conservatives, patient power goes much deeper and broader.

If you've ever tried to register with a GP you'll more than likely have found that it isn't as easy as you might expect it to be. Perhaps you've called your closest surgery to enquire about registering only to discover that you live just outside their catchment area and that the surgery you have to join is quite a bit further away. Or maybe when you called you were told that the surgery was not registering new patients at that time. And if you're registered with a GP and don't like the practice and would like to register somewhere else, well, you're basically out of luck. And don't even think about trying to register at the practice closest to your place of work.

The Conservatives would change this absurd state of affairs and empower people to choose the GP practice that is most convenient to them. That might be the one that's nearest your work, it might be the one nearest your home or it might be one that sits between your home and your work. Crucially, people would be empowered to change their GP at any time.

What's more, the Conservatives would remove the present

barriers which prevent the opening of new GP surgeries. These restrictions are many and varied, but include, for example, the power enjoyed by primary care trusts to restrict the number and size of GP practices in their area, and the funding for GP surgery premises, which is weighted tremendously in favour of practices that already exist. As the Conservative Party puts it in its *The Patient Will See You Now* policy paper, 'where demand for a new GP surgery exists, then there should be no difficulties in establishing one'. Furthermore, to encourage GPs to open surgeries in deprived areas the Conservative Party would reward them by paying more per patient through a 'weighted capitation formula', and by taking account of the impact of relative circumstance in deprived areas on outcomes.

By increasing choice, the Conservatives would increase competition in two ways: Competition on service and competition on outcome. At the service level patients would no longer be beholden to the whims of their GP. If they want a surgery that is open particularly early in the morning or late at night they can choose a GP who provides that; if they want a GP who allows them to book appointments more than forty-eight hours in advance they can do that too. When it comes to service, patients would be calling the shots. At an outcome level, though, GPs would no longer have a captive audience. Thanks to publicly available information on other patients' healthcare experiences and the results of treatment, GPs would very quickly find that the results they achieve for their patients and the 'bedside manner' they display when dealing with patients would determine whether their practice flourishes or closes down. With patients able to move where they wish, GPs would have to provide the level of service patients expect.

But for GPs to provide the best service possible, they too have to be empowered; and that means controlling their patients' budget. Under a Conservative government, GPs would have absolute control over the budgets NHS patients are entitled to. In practice that would mean, as described in the *Renewal Plan*, 'the GP having the ability to advise the patient and to commission care on their behalf from any willing provider at NHS costs and at NHS standards'. This budgetary control would sit alongside the patients' right to choose where they receive their secondary care (a right that would be bolstered by the public availability of information on outcomes at, for example, different hospitals). As the same policy paper explains: 'Budget-holding is a natural guarantee of efficiency, ensuring money follows the patient and it is spent on frontline care rather than on bureaucracy.' On top of that, such a system ensures that a patient's GP remains constantly in charge of the patient's treatment and constantly in the loop.

First-rate hospitals for a first-rate health service

As pointed out by Andrew Lansley during his 2009 party conference speech, the number of people killed by hospital infections such as *C. diff.* and MRSA each year is almost three times higher than the number of deaths on Britain's roads. Since 1997 the number killed has increased sixfold. Decisive action is needed.

With a greater emphasis on outcomes, greater choice for patients and greater access to information, hospitals would be compelled to take more effective steps to deal with infections. But the Conservatives aren't content to rely on those incentives alone. On top of their outcomes-based approach they would further incentivise hospitals by ensuring that they are either not paid at all, or not paid in full, 'for treatment which leaves the patient with an infection like MRSA if this was preventable by proper cleaning or isolation'.

Tied to this is the Conservative commitment to build 45,000 new single rooms in hospitals to ensure that anyone who wants to be can be accommodated on their own. As explained in the *Renewal Plan*, 'this is not simply a fickle preference. Many people object to having to stay in a mixed-sex ward in particular, for obvious reasons of privacy. But people also find their particular condition makes it uncomfortable to be in a ward with others, such as those in a state of discomfort or distress.' Similarly, the Conservatives have pledged to do away, once and for all, with mixed-sex wards. In committing to provide these additional single rooms, however, the Conservatives are mindful of the fact that three-quarters of hospitals do not currently have the capacity to isolate patients with hospital infections. By ensuring the delivery of these extra single rooms, the Conservatives would better equip the NHS to rise to the challenge of combating infections like *C. diff.* and MRSA.

Another key aspect of Conservative policy vis-à-vis the NHS is the commitment to stopping the closure of local A&E departments that has been driven forward by the Labour government. Similarly, the Conservatives have pledged to stop the closure of local maternity wards. Labour have favoured large, centralised maternity units over smaller local ones, but, as the Conservatives have pointed out, 'the evidence is that smaller maternity units tend to perform better'. On top of this the Conservatives have pledged to reverse Labour's reductions in health visitors and increase the number and frequency of health visits enjoyed by young families. For more on this see the Families chapter.

A final area that deserves attention is the Conservative Party's approach to purchasing drugs in the NHS. As the party has explained it:

> There is a new approach to offering new drugs to patients which allows drugs companies to launch new drugs through the NHS, but allows the NHS to only pay according to the benefits the drug brings to patients. This is known as value-based pricing . . . We should encourage the NHS to use whichever medicines are clinically effective, and agree to pay the drugs companies according to the therapeutic benefit

and innovative value . . . We will therefore negotiate the NHS's drug pricing mechanism to reflect this new value-based pricing.

This system of payment is described as offering 'the prospect of delivering greater benefits to patients for the same level of expenditure, thereby improving value for money and giving better rewards to companies to invest in the most valuable drugs.'

Taking politics out of healthcare

It's no secret that decisions regarding the NHS have far too often been made on political grounds rather than what's in the best interests of the country. One such example, outlined in the *Renewal Plan*, came when Peter Mandelson resigned as MP for Hartlepool. The local maternity unit had been earmarked for cuts, but when he resigned and provoked a by-election the Labour government reversed the decision to cut the maternity services. However, once the by-election was over and done with the decision was once again reversed and the maternity unit was closed down altogether.

To prevent such disgraceful politicking in the future, the Conservatives would create an independent NHS board (which would replace the NHS Executive, which is currently controlled by ministers). The board's responsibilities would include securing comprehensive health services, and delivering 'improvements in the physical and mental health of the population' and 'improvements in the diagnosis and treatment of illness'. Crucially, as explained in the *Renewal Plan*, 'to avoid creating political opportunities to manipulate the funding formula, NHS resource allocation should be set by the NHS Board, independently of ministers'.

Transport

From goods to people, our transport network quite literally keeps Britain moving. Better transport means a better society in almost every way. And when it comes to transport, the Conservative Party has made its mission very clear, as the shadow Secretary of State for Transport, Theresa Villiers MP, put it in her 2009 Conservative Party conference speech: 'Our mission is simple: to make transport safer, greener, more reliable and better value for money.' And in fulfilling that mission the Conservative approach to transport can be separated into three separate areas:

1. Aviation;
2. Improving rail travel;
3. Cutting congestion.

Aviation

Aviation makes an incredible contribution to the British economy, not just in terms of its direct economic impact but also in terms of the impact it has on British business by connecting us with the rest of the world. But as Villiers pointed out in a later 2009 speech, aviation is also 'one of the developed world's fastest growing sources of carbon emissions'. What's more, as Villiers has further observed, 'the historic annual growth rate [for the aviation industry] of around 5 per cent a year far outstrips the 1.5 per cent fuel efficiency savings which organisations from Rolls-Royce to the Tyndall Centre believe can be achieved'.

With this in mind the Conservative Party has been quite clear that the growth of the aviation industry cannot be made a higher priority than protecting the environment. That's not to say the Conservatives would stifle growth, rather they would expect the industry to accept that growth would have to proceed at a slower rate over the longer term. The environment simply cannot be sacrificed at the altar of air travel.

One priority is to encourage the industry to shift to newer aircraft, the most recent of which are up to 70 per cent more fuel efficient than their older counterparts. To achieve this the Conservative Party has committed to changing the system of taxes on aviation to flying these more environmentally friendly aircraft. Crucially, incentives would also be created for carriers to fly fuller planes.

Perhaps the boldest of the Conservative commitments in the field of aviation is its promise to block the building of a third runway at Heathrow and additional runways at Gatwick and Stansted. Not only has the financial case for the third runway not yet been made, but its environmental impact would undermine efforts to meet climate change commitments. And that's to say nothing about the impact on the millions of people who live in the vicinity. However, a Conservative government would (as described further below) give the go-ahead for high-speed rail links between Heathrow, London, Manchester, Birmingham and Leeds – and eventually to Newcastle and Scotland – creating an appealing alternative for thousands of short-haul flights. Indeed, as Villiers described in her conference speech, this 'could replace up to 66,500 flights a year'. Additional to this, though, the Conservatives would permit 'modest expansions' at regional airports to relieve some of the pressure on Gatwick, Stansted and Heathrow, provided, as Villiers describes, such expansions are 'reconcilable with local environmental factors and climate change concerns'.

Improving rail travel

Labour has resolutely failed when it comes to Britain's railways. Overcrowding is chronic; capacity has consistently failed to meet demand. As the Conservative Party's *Rail Review* policy paper makes clear: 'The most overcrowded trains on the network are running at over 170 per cent of capacity. And Network Rail predicts that passenger numbers will grow by 30 per cent over the next ten years.' What's more, on high-speed rail we are twenty years behind France. And incredibly, as a result of the Railways Act 2005, the government now has greater control over the railways than it did in the days of British Rail. Small wonder that things are in such a terrible state. A Conservative government would change this.

First, passengers would be put in control. Whereas at the moment rail users have no single body which they can approach to make complaints and to have disputes resolved, the Conservatives would hand greater power to the Office of Rail Regulation. As the Conservatives' policy paper explains: 'The changes we propose are aimed at allowing the regulator to bang heads together and take effective action against whichever organisation is responsible for the problems the passengers face.'

The powers of this newly reinforced regulator would include levying tougher sanctions on underperforming train operators and Network Rail, and even blocking bonuses to senior Network Rail executives where serious failures occur.

An area where a Conservative government would deliver massive and fundamental change is in high-speed rail. As indicated above, the Conservatives would give the go ahead for high-speed rail links between Heathrow, London, Manchester, Birmingham and Leeds – and eventually to Newcastle and Scotland. In terms of journey time the impact would be astonishing: to give just one example, the time taken to get by train from Manchester to Leeds would drop from 55 minutes to 17 minutes. And as the Conservatives have pointed out in the same policy paper:

As well as providing an attractive substitute for thousands of car journeys on some of the most congested motorways in the country, our proposal will help bring about a more balanced economy. By shrinking the distance between north and south we will help draw the Midlands and the north into the same growth zone as London and the south-east.

In terms of cost, the Conservatives believe the taxpayer would be restricted to meeting the cost of land and track, with the cost of construction and operating risks being covered by the private sector on the basis of expected returns.

The Conservatives would also dramatically reduce government involvement in the day-to-day running of the rail network. By way of example, that would mean civil servants would cease to set train timetables across the network, instead allowing train operators to set them in conjunction with Network Rail. Central government involvement at present levels is fundamentally counter-productive and has only exacerbated problems such as insufficient capacity. It's time that changed.

Cutting congestion

The Conservative Party is committed to addressing the problem of congestion on Britain's roads. At the macro level this would, in some instances, mean building new roads. And clearly, improved public transport has a critically important role to play. But the Conservatives are also determined to deliver a number of more minor changes to help address the problem. An example of this is the approach to traffic lights.

Without undermining the importance of traffic lights, it is clear that their overuse has a significant impact on congestion. Indeed, as Villiers pointed out in her 2009 congestion speech, even the Highways Agency has acknowledged that some traffic lights have been installed to 'impose delays'. With that in mind a Conservative government would give people the power to challenge the installation and phasing of traffic lights by granting them access to data underlying the decisions on traffic light placement and the timing of light changes. By opening up this kind of information much greater emphasis would be placed on the necessity of proposed traffic light placements and changes to phasing. Ultimately those in power would think twice before committing to new installations or phasing changes without solid justification.

And when it comes to road works, they inevitably cause serious congestion and all too often run massively over schedule. A Conservative government would impose much heavier fines for roadworks that overrun and, most radically, would make utility companies pay rent on any road space they dig up. As Villiers explains, they'll 'finally have an incentive to run their work efficiently'.

Finally, it is worth drawing attention to perhaps the most popular of all the Conservative transport policies, a commitment to not fund any new fixed speed cameras. Under Labour they've nearly trebled in number and they've failed to prove themselves as the best way to keep Britain's roads safe. Furthermore a Conservative government would make public the data on each existing speed camera's safety record and the fines it has generated. As Villiers explained, local communities would be able to 'judge for themselves whether a camera should stay or whether it should go'.

Climate change and energy security

The need for action to address climate change is both urgent and overwhelming. As William Hague has pointed out, it is one of the 'two greatest threats to humanity' (the other being nuclear proliferation). But even for those who doubt that climate change is real, the steps we must take at a national level to combat it (reducing carbon emissions) are in any event in our long-term interests by virtue of another threat to the UK: energy security. One need only consider Russia's desire to assert itself on the world stage to recognise that it is simply not in the UK's interests to be beholden to foreign powers for its energy needs – consider that at the present rate, almost 80 per cent of our gas will need to be imported by 2017. That means mitigating the effects and reducing our use of non-renewable energy sources whilst at the same time growing our use of renewables. Climate change and energy security may be very different problems, but the solution to both is exactly the same.

However, it has become only too obvious that Labour's reliance on targets has failed to yield the kind of drastic carbon emission reductions which are needed in the fight against climate change, and has done little to ensure an alternative domestic supply of energy to meet the challenge of energy security. Indeed, according to the Department for Environment Food and Rural Affairs' *Sustainable Development Indicators in your Pocket*, carbon emissions were almost unchanged between 1997 and 2007 (in fact increasing in several of those years) and fell by less than 2 per cent between 2007 and 2008.

Labour have failed on climate change and they have failed on energy security.

Evolving electricity

At the heart of the Conservative approach to tackling the twin threats of climate change and energy security is the understanding that, at a domestic level, the government alone cannot deliver the change which is needed. Accordingly, a Conservative government would focus its efforts on two things:

1. Establishing the infrastructure necessary for people to play their part in delivering a low carbon economy;
2. Delivering the necessary incentives to encourage people to play their part.

At the macro level, as will be seen further below, this would mean, to give but one example, radically overhauling the National Grid, transforming it from a system which is built around the principle of electricity being delivered by large and isolated power stations to one which enables decentralised generation by a myriad of new providers (including the family home).

Carbon capture and storage

Forty per cent of the UK's annual carbon emissions come from the electricity supply industry, and, as DEFRA have pointed out, the bulk of this comes from coal-fired power stations (which, like it or not, the UK will continue to rely on for some time). However, just because we are stuck with coal-fired power stations for the foreseeable future doesn't mean we have to accept the associated emissions. For example, tremendous strides have been made recently in carbon capture and storage (CCS) technology, so that it is now estimated, by the Commons Science and Technology Committee, that up to 85 per cent of a coal-fired power stations carbon emissions can be cut. But in order for CCS to work there needs to be somewhere to store the carbon and a way of transporting it to that location, something Labour have resolutely failed to address. A Conservative government would, as explained in *The Low Carbon Economy* policy paper, build pipelines to depleted gas fields in the North Sea (where carbon can be safely stored) from at least three of the UK's large coal-fired power stations. Crucially, the pipelines would be oversized to accommodate future expansion of the network for use by other power stations. This network would be paid for through receipts from the UK's auctioning of EU Emissions Trading Scheme (ETS) credits. Additionally a Conservative government would ensure that existing large-scale coal-fired power stations are converted to include CCS technology, and that those stations due to be built by 2020 are constructed with CCS technology in place. This would once again be paid for through ETS. And any additional large-scale coal-fired power stations which come to be proposed and signed off for construction would be required to incorporate CCS technology.

Marine power

The UK has incredible potential for offshore renewable energy generation. But as the Conservatives have pointed out, this potential is far from being fully realised. As with CCS, offshore generation suffers from a connectivity problem. As *The Low Carbon Economy* describes: 'The economies of new offshore wind plants are substantially affected by the need to construct elaborate and expensive connections to existing networks.' Whereas Labour have failed to address this obstacle, a Conservative government would simply amend the National Grid's regulations to require that they construct 'readily accessible under-sea direct current cables on the east and west coasts'. And to encourage the development of new marine electricity generation technologies, the Conservatives would use the Labour government's (unused) £50 million Marine Renewables Deployment Fund to create a series of 'marine energy parks' as incubators for innovation.

Nuclear power

Regardless of who forms the next government, new nuclear power stations will have to go ahead. However, the Conservatives have been utterly clear: for them, nuclear power is not a long-term solution to creating a low carbon economy and it's not an alternative to renewable technologies.

Good things come in small packages

As indicated above, the Conservative Party is committed to radically decentralising the energy network. The first hint of this was given in the section above on evolving electricity, but it is in the field of micro-generation that the true potential of this approach to delivering a low carbon economy becomes clear. As the party highlights in the above policy paper, thanks to new technology such as photovoltaic panels, combined heat and power and micro-hydro it is increasingly easy to generate electricity on a smaller scale. With that in mind a Conservative government would empower every home, business, school, community project and hospital in the country to generate electricity. At the moment, anyone wanting to take advantage of micro-generation technology will find immense obstacles in their way, such as the pain of a planning application. Rather than encourage people to generate their own electricity, Labour have actually discouraged it. A Conservative government would remove these obstacles and, moreover, would create a powerful incentive for people to start using micro-generation technology: a system of feed-in tariffs.

The operation of these tariffs would be straightforward. For example, if we assume a householder is generating electricity with photovoltaic panels, instead of receiving an electricity bill they would receive an 'electricity statement'. The statement would detail how much electricity they have consumed in the statement period and how much electricity they have generated. The amount consumed would be charged at the market price and the amount generated would be valued at a fixed long-term price per kilowatt-hour. Accordingly, the more the householder generated the lower their electricity bill would be. And if they generated more than they consume they could sell that extra electricity to their local network at the fixed price. Crucially, the electricity supplier's net costs in paying the micro-generation tariff would be met by the government (the Conservatives would cover this cost by abolishing the existing micro-generation grant programmes, which have acted as little more than barriers to entry). The net result of course is that homes, businesses, hospitals, schools and so on would begin to consume much more of their own electricity and much less of that produced by large-scale power stations relying on non-renewable energy sources. And to ensure that this system of micro-generation works to its full potential a Conservative government would legislate to require that anyone installing micro-generation technology be given a smart meter by their electricity supplier. Using this technology the user can monitor in real time how much electricity they are generating and how much they are consuming, thus creating a significant incentive to reduce their consumption. Indeed, as the Centre for Sustainable Energy has indicated, smart meters have the potential to cut energy consumption per user by up to 10 per cent.

Low-carbon transport

Driving forward change

The Conservative Party is committed to encouraging the development of a mass market for electric vehicles in the UK. And for good reason. As the Conservatives have pointed out, if the current fleet of cars on Britain's roads were replaced with equivalent electric ones, the UK's carbon emissions would go down by an astonishing 22 per cent.

Clearly, any effort to transfer drivers from traditional vehicles to electric ones will require the government to set long-term targets for the car industry to reduce emissions from the vehicles they produce. But the larger impediment for the development of electric cars, and the biggest hurdle in establishing a mass market for them, is the fact that there are very few charging points for them in the UK. To address this problem a Conservative government would designate electric car charging points as 'regulated assets'. By doing this, distribution network operators could, as we explain, 'invest ahead of need and cover the installation costs'.

High-speed rail
The Conservatives see the development of high-speed rail as a fundamental part of the battle to reduce carbon emissions (for example by reducing the number of short-haul flights). See the chapter on Transport for more.

Strong as houses

Ensuring that homes are effectively insulated is critically important in the battle to reduce carbon emissions. Accordingly the Conservatives have pledged to provide a grant to households of up to £6,500 for approved home efficiency works.

Working internationally

Finally, whilst it's important that the UK does all it can to reduce its own carbon emissions, the battle against climate change will not be won without international cooperation. Without it, individual efforts to reduce carbon emissions will be futile. The Conservatives recognise this and have accordingly made clear that climate change would be a foreign policy priority for a Conservative government. For more on this see the chapters on Foreign Policy and International Development.

The countryside

To anyone who treasures the countryside and recognises its inherent value – a value which transcends cold economics – the years of Labour government since 1997 have been a tragedy. Whether one thinks of the 200 rural schools lost since 1997, the 1,400 rural post offices lost since 2000, the 384 rural police stations shut down in Labour's first two terms of office, the unrelenting barrage of inspections and form-filling foisted upon farmers, or indeed simply the hunting ban enacted only to facilitate a class war, it is clear that the Labour Party holds the countryside in little more than contempt.

The time has come for change. In October 2009 the shadow Secretary of State for Environment, Food and Rural Affairs, Nick Herbert MP, said:

> As Conservatives we believe in the inherent value of conserving things. We know the importance of securing a good future for successive generations. We also know that our countryside matters. It matters for our health and wellbeing. It matters for our wildlife. It matters for food production. It matters in our response to climate change. It matters for its intrinsic beauty. So we value the countryside . . . Our task is to ensure that government, society, communities and individuals value it too.

Rural development

The UK's population is growing, the Office of National Statistics estimating that by 2033 it will reach 71 million. And more people means a need for more houses. But Labour, rather than entrusting local people with the power to determine the placement and number of additional houses needed, have characteristically rendered them impotent by simply dictating what will be built where. For example, Labour's 'South East Plan' has ordered that 650,000 additional houses be built in the region over the next two decades. What's more, the plan goes further by, as Nick Herbert has explained, setting 'a requirement of over 100,000 new houses for the two regions of East Kent & Ashford and Kent Thames Gateway'. But Labour don't stop there in tying the hands of local people; on top of regional planning, they have empowered central government civil servants to force specific house-building targets on every local authority in the country through so-called 'regional spatial strategies'.

A Conservative government would return power to the hands of local people; trusting them to ensure that the necessary houses are built to accommodate the growing numbers in their own communities. To achieve this, the Conservatives have pledged to scrap all regional planning and regional spatial strategies. Instead, the decision on what houses to build and where would be taken by local authorities, accountable to as ever to local people. And to incentivise the building of new houses a Conservative government would, as Herbert describes, '[match] the additional council tax raised by each council for each new house build for each of the six years after that house is built'.

One additional example of Labour's disregard for the opinion of the people in the countryside is the Infrastructure Planning Commission (IPC), a quango which ostensibly exists to speed up planning applications for large-scale infrastructure builds. Needless to say, it does this by taking the power to make these decisions away from the elected local authorities which will be affected by the proposed builds. The Conservative solution to this is simple: abolish the IPC.

Local services

As indicated above, Labour's assault on local services in the country-side has been relentless. A Conservative government would take a different approach.

For example, as discussed in the Health chapter of this book, whereas Labour have favoured large centralised maternity units over smaller local ones, the Conservatives have pledged to stop Labour's closures. Alongside this, a Conservative government would protect family doctor services.

When it comes to schools, our policy is very clear: local people will be in charge. So whereas Labour have made it their mission to close rural schools, a Conservative government would grant parents the power to set up their own schools in the local area (see the chapter on Schools for more).

To give one final example of the difference between the Labour approach and the one a Conservative government would take, the value of rural post offices would not be measured in terms of their economic viability, but rather in the wider public and social value they bring to an area.

Supporting farmers

The primary industry of the countryside is farming, and it always will be. A Conservative government would give farmers the support they need. And first and foremost that means completely reforming farming regulations to, as the Conservative Party website puts it, 'lift the burden of unnecessary paperwork and inspections'. But that's only the start.

One of the greatest challenges we will face as a nation in the future is food shortages. With the world's population estimated to increase by three billion people by 2050 we simply can't be sure that British people will be able to sustain themselves on imported food. Whereas Labour's view has been that it simply doesn't matter where we get our food from, the Conservative Party is clear, as Nick Herbert explained in the 2009 speech cited above, 'that it should be a strategic priority of government to increase domestic food production in order to safeguard our food security'.

For a Conservative government, a first step in supporting farmers to grow and sell more food would be to ensure better labelling for food products through our own Honest Food Campaign. Too often food is ambiguously labelled, suggesting something was grown or reared in the UK when in fact it wasn't. To encourage the purchase of British food, a Conservative government would work to ensure British people knew exactly where their food was coming from.

The second step for a Conservative government would be to harness the buying power of the public sector. Currently, the public sector spends over £2 billion every year on food. Yet all too often that food is foreign in origin. Accordingly, the Conservative Party has committed to ordering all government departments to purchase only food that, in Herbert's words, 'meets British standards wherever it can be achieved [and] that will mean more local food'.

Hunting ban

The Conservative Party has never relented in making the point that the Hunting Act, brought in by Labour, is a terrible piece of legislation which should be repealed. Accordingly, a Conservative government would, as Herbert detailed in an earlier October 2009 speech, 'give Parliament the opportunity to repeal the Hunting Act on a free vote'.

Europe

It's no secret that the UK's relationship with the EU has in the past been the cause of great internal strife within the Conservative Party. Indeed, it is as a direct result of that historical strife that Labour has taken every opportunity in the build-up to the general election to create the impression that these same divides plague the Conservative Party today. But whereas such accusations may have rung true in the past, it is abundantly clear that the modern Conservative Party under David Cameron is one with a settled position on the EU. The party's *European Election Manifesto* makes this clear: 'The Conservatives are committed to Britain's membership of the EU. We are proud of the EU's achievements, such as progress made in widening the freedom to do business, travel and find work, and in anchoring democracy and stability across the continent.'

But just because the modern Conservative Party is at ease with the UK's membership in the EU, that does not mean it has bought into the European federalist project which would see an ever-increasing centralisation of power in Brussels and an unrelenting loss of sovereignty on the part of member states. As Cameron made clear in his 2009 speech 'A Europe Policy that People Can Believe In', 'we believe Britain's interests are best served by membership of a European Union that is an association of its member states. We will never allow Britain to slide into a federal Europe.' Nowhere is this clearer than with the Conservatives' position on the Lisbon Treaty.

Protecting Britain's interests: the Lisbon Treaty

If one stain on Labour's record in power stands out above all others it is quite probably the failure to follow through on their manifesto commitment to give the British people a referendum on the EU Constitution. For whilst Labour may claim that the Lisbon Treaty was a different animal from the original constitution which the French and Dutch people rejected, leaders across Europe were all too open in explaining that Lisbon was little more than the Constitution by another name. By failing to provide a referendum on Lisbon the Labour government failed to fulfil their promise to the British people. Labour gave their word and without a second thought, they broke it.

The lesson learned from the Lisbon Treaty was that the British people need additional protection from the whims of their government. They need a guarantee that additional powers will only ever be transferred to Europe following their agreement in a referendum. David Cameron said in 2009: 'It is not politicians' power to give away – it belongs to the people.' With that in mind, Cameron has pledged a 'referendum lock', similar to that enjoyed by the Irish people, which fulfils this need.

As a second measure to protect Britain's interests, particularly in light of the Lisbon Treaty, the Conservative Party would introduce a United Kingdom Sovereignty Bill, which would, in Cameron's words, 'make it clear that ultimate authority stays in this country, in our parliament . . . It is about an assurance that the final word on our laws is here in Britain.' Such a piece of legislation is not unusual amongst our European neighbours; Germany for example has such protection under its constitution. Ultimately this piece of legislation is about making sure that British courts never, for any reason, come to regard any European authority as being higher than Parliament in Westminster.

Perhaps the most worrying aspect of the Lisbon Treaty, though, is the so-called 'ratchet clauses', which contain a mechanism to do away with all-important vetoes and are designed to allow the transfer of yet more power to the EU without the need for further treaties. Clearly, such clauses are anti-democratic and an offence to not just the British but the people of all the EU member states, who should have ultimate say over any transfer of their country's power. Cameron's response to these disgraceful clauses has been robust: 'We do not believe that any of these so-called ratchet clauses should be used to hand over more powers from Britain to the EU . . . We would change the law so that any use of a ratchet clause by a future government would require full approval by Parliament.'

But as Cameron has pointed out, these guarantees are designed to prevent problems arising in the future. They are not about addressing serious problems which we face here and now. For that reason, the Conservative Party has outlined additional pledges designed to address some of the most pressing issues in the UK's relationship with the EU.

First and foremost, being mindful of the impact of Labour's decision to give up Britain's opt-out from the Social Chapter, the Conservatives have pledged to negotiate the return of the opt-out from EU social and employment legislation 'in those areas which have proved most damaging to our economy and public services'. An illustrative example of the impact of EU social and employment legislation is the Working Time Directive, which has caused tremendous problems for the NHS, by reducing the amount of frontline staff time available for care, and hampered efforts to keep Britain moving during the cold spell in January by curtailing the amount of time road gritters could work. The need for an opt-out is overwhelming, and the Conservative Party would ensure that it is achieved.

On top of this the Conservatives have pledged to negotiate for a return of powers in the field of criminal justice. Put simply, there exists a serious threat that EU judges will gain increasing control over criminal justice in the UK. This could mean increasing jurisdiction for the European Court of Justice in matters of criminal law and, most worryingly, the power of the EU to initiate criminal investigations in the UK. A Conservative government would prevent this.

Supporting Britain by supporting business

As the Conservatives have explained, the single market, with its four freedoms of movement of goods, capital, services and labour, is crucial to the UK's economic success. Accordingly, a Conservative government will be relentless in working to open up new markets, will push for a new test to be applied to any new EU legislation to ensure that it does not weaken the single market.

And because the Conservative Party is pro-business, it is also pro-EU enlargement. As the European election manifesto highlighted: 'Trade between the UK and the ten countries that joined the EU in 2004 increased by almost 400 per cent between 1992 and 2005, ten times the rate of growth in trade between the UK and the rest of the world.' A larger EU means a more prosperous UK. But enlarging the EU won't in and of itself guarantee a more prosperous future for UK business. The Conservatives are therefore committed to pressing for a new test to be applied to all new EU legislation to ensure that small businesses are not disproportionately or adversely affected by it. We will also fight existing regulation which places too much restriction on British business, and will strive to enforce a 'sunset clause' on EU legislation, which would require it to be 'reviewed or repealed after a specific period' so as to ensure that the volume of regulation is never allowed to grow unchecked.

Of critical importance is the Conservative commitment to protect the City of London from any and all attempts by the EU to restrict its ability to function as a global financial centre. As the leader of the Conservatives in the European Parliament, Timothy Kirkhope MEP, warned: 'London must never be placed at a competitive disadvantage to other financial districts.' The City's importance to the UK economy is unparalleled and for that reason a Conservative government would be uncompromising in protecting it.

Building trust in the EU

The Conservatives are committed to building trust in Europe by confronting those aspects of the EU which are, rightly, the source of much suspicion. At the heart of our approach is a commitment to transparency. For example, the Conservative Party will fight for a requirement that, as explained in the European manifesto, the European Commission 'be subject to an enhanced code of conduct for commissioners, including the requirement to list not only any gifts they receive (at present only those over €150) but also whom they are from, and to register all hospitality over €250, again with details of the donor'. A corollary of this commitment to transparency is the further commitment to ensuring that citizens throughout the EU have access to documents across EU institutions through freedom of information requests (just as is the case in the UK).

Defence, Afghanistan and terrorism

At present there are more than 41,000 British service personnel deployed in thirty-two countries and overseas territories. Far away from the coffee shops, pubs, clubs, cinemas and restaurants on our high streets, British troops are doing the business of keeping the

UK safe. And as we've learned only too well over the past decade – from 9/11 to 7/7 to Afghanistan – the world is perhaps more dangerous now than it ever has been in the past. Where once the threats we faced were well delineated, we now face a much wider range of threats, which includes the uncertainty of an enemy that is not confined by any borders or beholden to any of the rules of war, or indeed humanity, which dictate our own behaviour. In September 2009 the shadow Secretary of State for Defence, Liam Fox MP, gave a snapshot of what he described as the 'deteriorating global security environment', focusing on the following issues:

- In Pakistan, a country armed with nuclear weapons and which already contends with terrible political and military instability, the Taliban has 'reached an operational distance of within 60 miles of Islamabad'.

- Russia is increasingly flexing its muscle internationally and is rearming on an incredible scale. [As Fox pointed out in a March 2009 speech, Russia has committed to spending $200 billion by 2015 to upgrade its armed forces, and is building six new nuclear-powered aircraft carriers, eight ballistic missile submarines and 'the largest nuclear icebreakers in the world' for use in its operations in the Arctic. With regard to the Arctic specifically, Russia has further raised tensions in an arena which already offers the potential for serious armed conflict by declaring its intention to annex some 460,000 square miles of territory believed to be amongst the Arctic's richest in oil and gas.] Furthermore, and perhaps most worrying of all, as Fox describes, 'we now have Russian strategic bombers probing British airspace again – something that occurred on a regular basis during the Cold War'.

- Iran, in an unprecedented move, deployed six warships in the Gulf of Aden earlier this summer, is on the verge of acquiring a nuclear weapon, continues with its missile tests and continues to export terrorism.

- North Korea has continued its programme of missile tests, has tested its second nuclear bomb and, as Fox describes, 'has torn up the armistice that brought to an end the 1950–53 Korean War'.

Fox's snapshot merely scratches the surface of the unparalleled dangers that face the United Kingdom right now. And yet, despite these dangers, Labour have treated defence with nothing short of contempt. We have had four Defence Secretaries in four years and the current one is ranked twenty-first out of the twenty-three members of the Cabinet. The government-commissioned Gray Review of MoD procurement concluded that the UK's defence equipment programme is underfunded by a shocking £35 billion and running five years behind schedule. In 2004, with British forces engaged in Afghanistan and Iraq, Gordon Brown cut £1.4 billion from the helicopter budget, leading inevitably to a tremendous shortage for troops in both theatres. So serious was the effect of this shortage that the Queen herself was reported to have rebuked the Prime Minister.

But the most damning fact of all when it comes to Labour's reckless disregard shown for defence is that the last Strategic Defence Review (SDR) took place twelve years ago. As a result, as Liam Fox has pointed out, 'the armed forces are working on assumptions based on a world before 9/11, before the Iraq War and before Afghanistan'. Without more recent SDRs, the Labour government have failed to ensure that Britain's armed forces are equipped and structured to deal with a world which is radically different from the one in 1998.

Labour have unequivocally and fundamentally failed on defence. Change is desperately needed if the UK is to be able to confidently confront and see off the threats which it faces right now and those it will inevitably face in the years ahead. And when it comes to delivering the level of change required, only the Conservative Party has the requisite policies, resolve and commitment to see it through.

Getting defence right at the macro level

A Conservative government would immediately launch an SDR upon coming into office and, moreover, would legislate to ensure that one is held every four to five years. In a rapidly changing world the stakes are too high to ever permit another government to treat the need for regular SDRs with the disdain shown by Labour.

The role of the SDR would be five-fold:

1. To define the UK's strategic interests and where they exist at home and abroad;
2. To assess the strategic environment and threats to those interests, so far as can reasonably be predicted;
3. To determine the military capabilities needed to protect those interests;
4. To review the current programmes and shape of Britain's armed forces to determine if they can deliver those capabilities;
5. To take account of prevailing budgetary constraints

Until an SDR has actually been carried it simply won't be possible to determine what changes are needed in the armed forces and beyond to ensure the UK is able to meet its defence needs.

On top of the SDR, though, a Conservative government would also tackle the problems with defence procurement. As Fox puts it: 'We will perform a root and branch reform of the [defence] procurement process. Under a Conservative government the procurement process will be the servant, not the master, of the SDR.'

To achieve this, and in so doing to address the 'endemic' failure identified by the damning Gray Review, the Conservatives would ensure that the defence procurement process had four main objectives. As outlined by Fox, these are:

1. 'To provide the best possible equipment to our armed forces when they need it, where they need it and at a reasonable cost to the taxpayer';

2. 'To use defence procurement to underpin Britain's strategic relationships' – for example by ensuring closer cooperation with the United States;

3. 'To provide better stability to the armed forces and better predictability to the defence industry' – regular SDRs will be central to this;

4. 'To preserve UK defence jobs by maximising exports'.

Trident

There are those who doubt whether Trident should be replaced. Their argument is that the world today is very different to the one during the Cold War, that terrorists will not be deterred by our nuclear arsenal in the way the Soviet Union was. But this argument neglects one very important point: the uncertainty of the future. With a resurgent Russia, an Iranian government determined to get a nuclear weapon and North Korea making its aspirations for long-range nuclear capability all too clear, who knows what kind of threat we will face in ten, twenty, thirty or fifty years' time. And that is precisely why Britain can't afford to do away with its nuclear deterrent, and particularly why we can't afford to do away with a submarine-based deterrent which provides the ultimate guarantee that the UK will always be able to strike back against her enemies. Accordingly, a Conservative government would back, in Fox's words, 'a round-the-clock, submarine-based nuclear deterrent'.

Afghanistan

It's no secret that the war in Afghanistan is losing public support. But the repercussions of pulling our troops out too early, before the task is complete, don't bear thinking about. It's quite clear that without the presence of Western troops, Afghanistan with its current security infrastructure would be retaken by the Taliban almost immediately and would once again become an unrestricted training ground for al-Qaeda. Even putting aside the direct threat this would pose to the UK and the West more generally, the threat to regional stability is all too apparent. Nuclear-armed Pakistan, for example, which, as we have seen, is already contending with Taliban operations within 60 miles of its capital, would face a renewed and re-emboldened threat from those elements determined to make the most of the instability that already exists in the country.

Afghanistan is the frontline in the fight against global terror. Accordingly, under a Conservative government, it would be the main military effort of the UK. Indeed, there is no better example of the seriousness with which the Conservatives take the war in Afghanistan than David Cameron's open disagreement with President Barack Obama's decision to set a pull-out date for US troops.

Crucially, though, whereas Labour have demonstrated their willingness to commit to war regardless of public opinion, and have consistently failed to articulate the reasons for the UK's deployment in Afghanistan, the Conservatives have recognised from the beginning that the war can only be won by earning the support of the British people. And as Liam Fox has pointed out, that means doing a much better job of defining what 'winning' actually means in the Afghan context, and what steps must be taken to get there. Indeed, even in opposition the Conservatives have begun this process, as Fox made plain: 'Success will be achieved when we have a stable enough Afghanistan to exercise its own sovereignty and to manage its own internal and external security free from outside interference.'

The Conservatives have also not shied away from making clear that in government they would expect those NATO allies who have allowed the US and the UK to carry the main burden of troop deployment to contribute to the cost of that deployment. As Fox said in December 2009: 'Why should the few carry the many? Common security implies common commitment. It is quite wrong for everyone in the street to get the same insurance policy when only a few pay the premiums.'

Furthermore, given the tremendous numbers of additional troops the US has committed to Afghanistan, David Cameron has made clear that he will push for British forces to be 'more concentrated in areas where [they] can make a difference'. At the moment in Helmand British forces are responsible for about two-thirds of the population, whilst almost double the number of American troops are responsible for the remaining third. Clearly, this isn't an equitable or indeed even a strategically sensible settlement. A Conservative government would push to have this situation addressed.

Finally, with regard to troop welfare, the Conservatives have committed to doubling the bonuses paid to troops serving in Afghanistan and, perhaps more importantly, changing the rules so that a soldier's leave will be calculated from when he or she arrives home rather than when he or she leaves base. (For the Conservative approach to the Military Covenant, see below.)

Terrorism

As indicated above, international terrorism is one of the greatest threats to the UK today, and it is one which will persist long into the future. But whereas fighting a conventional war is largely a matter confined to the capabilities of our armed forces and intelligence services, it is plain to see that the fight against terror requires a multi-faceted approach. And for this reason, it is a task well suited to the Conservative Party's approach to government in general, which recognises that, to use a different example, addressing the rise of violent crime is as much about support for families and educational policy as it is about criminal justice.

It will therefore come as no surprise to hear that under a Conservative government international development would play a key role in addressing some of the root causes of radicalism:

extreme poverty, deprivation, political instability and so on (see the International Development chapter for more). Additionally, the Conservatives have drawn a link between radicalism and climate change, in that climate change can, for example, lead to a scarcity of resources and, as a result, regional instability, economic hardship etc. – the perfect environment for radicalism (for more on this see the Foreign Policy chapter). For the Conservatives, terrorism doesn't exist in isolation and as a result our response to terrorism would be multi-dimensional.

And just as the UK's response to terrorism must be multi-faceted, so there must be a recognition that the UK does not exist in splendid isolation. To defeat terrorism we must work with the international community. So whilst the shadow Security Minister, Baroness Neville-Jones, has made clear that the Conservative Party supports the UK's current counter-terrorism strategy, a Conservative government would nevertheless seek to build on that strategy by helping other countries to learn the lessons of its success. To give but one example, this would mean working with other countries to help them develop the kind of integrated police–intelligence approach to terrorist investigations which have proven so successful in the UK.

Defeating terrorism is a long-term commitment, it will not be an easy fight to win, and there will be costs along the way. But we will only be successful if we ensure a truly joined-up approach to terror at the domestic level and a philosophy of cooperation and sharing best practice at the international level. A Conservative government would deliver just that.

The Military Covenant

The Military Covenant is in a sorry state. From housing – where, as the Conservative Party's Military Commission pointed out, 45 per cent of UK single living accommodation and 56 per cent of overseas single living accommodation is graded at four on a four-point scale – to healthcare, the nation's moral obligation to its servicemen and women is not being fulfilled. Perhaps the must damning and illustrative figure of all is that whilst 255 service personnel were killed in action in the Falklands War, an astonishing 264 have committed suicide since. As Liam Fox said: 'We cannot allow the same tragedy to be repeated for those who have served in the Gulf, in Iraq, or in Afghanistan.'

A Conservative government would dedicate itself to repairing the covenant.

Foreign policy

When it comes to voting at a general election, foreign policy tends to be one of those areas that ranks low on people's list of priorities. The issues involved in the execution of foreign policy can often seem less pressing, less urgent, than matters such as health, education and the economy. Nevertheless, the Conservative Party has never shied from placing its approach to foreign policy front and centre and from making the case for how critically important those issues affected by foreign policy are to the United Kingdom's safety and wellbeing, and therefore to the UK's ability to flourish in all those other areas which tend to be higher on people's priority lists.

In defining the Conservative approach to foreign policy, the party's website states:

A Conservative government's approach to foreign affairs will be based on liberal Conservative principles. Liberal, because Britain must be open and engaged with the world, supporting human rights and championing the cause of democracy and the rule of law at every opportunity. But Conservative, because our policy must be hard headed and practical, dealing with the world as it is and not as we wish it were.

The corollary of this approach is that a Conservative government would completely reject the notion that the UK can only exert its influence on the world stage by acting through the European Union. For sure, there will be times, very often in fact, when it is only right that we act in tandem with our European partners to exert influence over particular issues at play in the international arena.

But as an independent nation it is only right that where appropriate we act in our own national interest, independently of the EU. Whereas the Labour Party is committed to an ever-increasing union and, as evidenced by its failure to provide a referendum on the Lisbon Treaty, to a more federal Europe, the Conservative Party remains the only party that will defend British interests above all others. This commitment to working through Europe when appropriate, and to working independently when not, is evidence of that. Crucially, though, working independently does not necessarily mean working unilaterally, as will be seen below.

As William Hague explained in a 2009 speech, the UK's ability to act independently as well as through the EU on matters of foreign policy is rendered all the more important by 'the two greatest threats to human welfare and peace in our generation – nuclear proliferation and climate change'. If we are to address these challenges it is imperative that the UK, to paraphrase Hague, reinforces its engagement with the rest of the world. To support such engagement and to ensure the UK is able to exert its influence on the world stage effectively the Conservative Party has adopted five themes which would guide the party's approach to foreign affairs when in government.

Before explaining those themes in more detail, though, it is worthwhile expanding upon the nature of the threat presented, in a foreign policy context, by nuclear non-proliferation and climate change. For in understanding that threat, it becomes clear why the Conservative Party's approach to foreign policy is needed now more than ever.

Nuclear non-proliferation

Baroness Neville-Jones, the shadow Security Minister, explained in October 2009:

> For over three years the Conservative Party has warned of an approaching crisis in the global nuclear non-proliferation regime. This crisis has been mounting as the result of the actions of countries like Iran, . . . the thriving nuclear black market, the growing nexus between proliferation and non-state actors (including terrorists) and stalemate over the future of the Nuclear Non-Proliferation Treaty [NPT].

The example given of Iran is perhaps the most illustrative of the threat and challenges we face in the arena of non-proliferation. On the surface Iran claims to be pursuing civil nuclear power, which, as Neville-Jones has pointed out, is perfectly within its rights provided it is done in accordance with NPT and International Atomic Energy Agency rules. But the secrecy and cheating surrounding Iran's programme and the discovery of a hidden facility in Qom raises even further the probability that Iran is actively trying to develop nuclear weapons. Needless to say the ramifications of a nuclear Iran in the latter sense don't bear thinking about. And yet, as Neville-Jones made clear, a very real threat exists that the NPT will not be renewed:

The entire credibility of the NPT is at stake. Imagine the consequences if it is not renewed. A world of nuclear blackmail that puts the rule of law in international relations at severe risk. It would undermine the policies and structures for the management of international affairs that the Western world has sought to build up since the Second World War. Even if it did not result in the horror of nuclear engagement it would present a challenge to Western – specifically but not only American – leadership, the like of which we have not hitherto experienced. The Gulf and the Middle East generally would not just be an unstable place. It would be highly dangerous, with the risk of a nuclear arms race and further proxy activity.

The importance of the UK's role in ensuring agreement on the NPT cannot be overstated, and the repercussions that would follow from failure are so dire as to be almost beyond contemplation. Returning to the Iran example, a failure to renew the NPT could only lead to one thing: an Iran armed with nuclear weapons, and all the implications that come with such a reality. The stakes could not be higher.

Of course, as we already know, even with the NPT in force there is no way of guaranteeing that Iran will be prevented from gaining nuclear weapons; but it does ensure a legitimate legal basis upon which to oppose Iran's development of those weapons. Once again, though, the role of the UK government in ensuring that the worst possible conclusion is avoided could not be more critical. The situation requires careful negotiation – both formal and informal – with Iran, it requires the building of a powerful international coalition in support of robust sanctions to be deployed if Iran refuses to yield to negotiation, it requires getting the UN Security Council to agree to sanctions to be imposed on Iran if and when necessary (no mean feat when one considers that China has valuable oil contracts with Iran and Russia places such importance on arms exports). And it requires creating a credible alternative for Iran, a means by which nuclear power can be provided to Iran without Iran having to enrich uranium itself. All told, addressing the nuclear proliferation challenge presented by Iran alone is as complicated as the ramifications of failing in this endeavour are terrifying.

Climate change

There already exists in this book a chapter that deals specifically with the Conservative Party's approach to climate change (which naturally places emphasis on international cooperation), and for that reason the subject will not be covered in much detail here. However, there are certain aspects of the threats posed by climate change that should be borne in mind when considering the importance of effective foreign policy.

According to research by the independent organisation International Alert there are an alarming forty-six countries at risk from violent conflict as a direct result of climate change, and a further fifty-six face a high risk of instability. As William Hague said in a 2009 speech focusing on the connection between foreign policy and climate change, this creates the very real potential of the developing and developed worlds being brought into conflict as a result of climate change.

What's more, as Hague further explains:

> Environmental change also has implications for the balance of global and regional power, and we may witness charged competition between countries over resources. Israel and her Arab neighbours have been disputing limited water supplies over decades. In this region 5 per cent of the world's population share 1 per cent of the water supply and countries such as Iraq, Syria and Jordan and parts of Turkey and Lebanon are already suffering from acute drought.

On top of this, developed countries will find that they have to 'compete for dwindling energy supplies, along with other nations, as long as fossil fuels remain essential to economic activity'. Hague goes on to point out: 'This will strengthen the hand of energy-producing governments in international affairs, whilst weakening our own position – to the detriment of foreign policy in instances where these nations do not share our values.'

The five foreign policy themes of a Conservative government

As indicated above, Conservative Party foreign policy would be guided by five themes designed to ensure that the UK engages effectively with the rest of the world and that it is able to exert its influence on the world stage.

Firstly, the Conservative Party recognises that just as international problems demand a combined response on the part of many nations, so too do they demand a combined domestic response on the part of many different government departments. An issue that affects the Foreign Office is likely to have implications for the Ministry of Defence and the Home Office, for example. Accordingly, a Conservative government would create a National Security Council (NSC) in order to, as William Hague outlined in his October 2009 speech, 'integrate at the highest levels of government the work of our Foreign, Defence, Energy, Home and International Development departments.' Astonishingly, the Labour Party's equivalent (which was created in response to the Conservative proposal), the National Security Committee, only met on three occasions over a period of twenty-one months and, as Hague critiqued, 'despite two wars being in progress'. The Conservatives' NSC would meet regularly and ensure, as Hague described, 'that ministers will take the big decisions together, with all the information, and follow through in every single department.'

The second theme is a commitment to the transatlantic alliance.

The importance of the relationship with the United States cannot be overstated. As Hague made clear in the same speech, the alliance is 'necessary as much as ever in the coming year to bring success in May at the review conference of the Non-Proliferation Treaty, and to deter and dissuade Iran from the final development of nuclear weapons'.

Thirdly, the Conservatives are committed to deepening the UK's alliances beyond the United States and Europe. Under a Conservative government, emphasis would accordingly be placed on developing the UK's relationship with India, creating a more 'effective' relationship with China and ensuring support for democracy and stability in Pakistan. Additionally, as Hague explains, it means 'using our coordination of our domestic departments to elevate entire national relationships, in culture, commerce and education as well as in diplomacy, with nations in the Gulf, and others in North Africa or Latin America.' Only by building stronger and wider alliances and partnerships can the major international challenges be met.

The fourth theme is a commitment to reforming older international institutions like the UN to make them more effective for the world as it is today, not as it was decades ago. But equally, a Conservative government would work to see that greater use is made of the latent potential in newer institutions like the G20.

Finally, a Conservative government is committed quite simply to leading by example. As William Hague says:

Given the growth of the power of nations that do not share all our assumptions on the great value of freedom and democracy, and the relative shrinking of Britain's and Europe's economic weight, we must all the more uphold our own values, doing so not by imposing them on others but by being an inspiring example of them ourselves. The country that drove the slave trade from the seas 200 years ago can still be one of the greatest forces for common humanity.

Whilst this last theme may seem less robust than the others, it is nevertheless perhaps the most important. Only by living our values can we hope to retain and maintain our credibility on the world stage, and to influence international events for the better. For the Conservative Party this will act as a guiding light in the execution of Britain's foreign policy. Rightly so.

International development

The commitment by the Conservatives to increase spending on the NHS in real terms year on year is unlikely to cause any controversy, but the party's commitment to increasing spending on international development is another matter entirely, not least when it is only the international aid and the NHS budgets which are guaranteed to avoid cuts in light of the UK's historic deficit. Unsurprisingly, there are those who wonder whether we should look after ourselves before we look after other people. Ultimately, though, even if this Conservative commitment is not the most popular, it is nevertheless right.

The justification for increasing Britain's aid budget is, as the Conservative Party website makes clear, two-fold: there is a moral imperative and a practical imperative.

The moral case for increased spending is only too clear. As Andrew Mitchell MP, shadow International Development Secretary, said in October 2009: 'Here in Britain we are living in an age of austerity. Times are tough. We are having to tighten our belts. But out there in the developing world times are infinitely tougher.' And these aren't just hollow words, as our *One World Conservatism* policy paper describes:

> 9.2 million children die before the age of five each year. Two million die on the day they are born – and 500,000 women die at childbirth. A third of children in Africa suffer brain damage as a result of malnutrition. 72 million children are missing out on an education. Every day 30,000 children die from easily preventable diseases. That's 21 children every minute. 33 million people are infected with HIV/AIDS. There are 11 million AIDS orphans in Africa. Every hour, 300 people become infected with HIV and 225 people die from AIDS – and 25 of these are children.

The global economic downturn only makes the plight of those in the world's developing countries even worse. Now more than ever they are in need of international aid.

But alongside the moral imperative sits the practical imperative, all too often forgotten, as pointed out on the Conservative Party's website: 'Failed and impoverished states are incubators of disease, insecurity and extremism, and so present a clear threat to our national interest.' An example given by Mitchell serves to reinforce this point well:

> The terrorists who tried to blow up airliners over the Atlantic were part of a global network of terror which thrives on conflict, poverty and instability from Pakistan to Somalia. So while global poverty is an affront to our morality, it is also a clear and present danger to British lives and British interests.

But unlike the Labour government, the Conservative Party does not see increased spending as an end in itself. It's results that count. Under Labour the misuse of aid money has been astonishing, from the £240,000 that was given as a grant to help set up a Brazilian dance troupe in Hackney to the £38 million of aid given to China, a country which, as Mitchell pointed out in the above speech, 'spent £20 billion on hosting the Olympics'. And incredibly, aid has even been given to Russia, a country which, as Mitchell highlighted, 'has a GDP of over a trillion dollars and is a member of the G8'. Clearly, things have to change. Whilst a Conservative government would spend more, it would also spend better.

Firstly, a Conservative government would review the 100-plus countries which currently receive aid to determine which should continue receiving it. Clearly, China and Russia would be the first to be struck off the list.

But perhaps more importantly, the Conservatives would create an 'Independent Aid Watchdog' to, as *One World Conservatism* explains it, 'ensure the impartial and objective analysis of the effectiveness of British aid'. Labour's system of self-evaluation simply isn't rigorous enough. A Conservative government would ensure, particularly in light of the commitment to increasing the international aid budget, that every pound of taxpayers' money achieves demonstrable and effective results.

To further embed this culture of taxpayer value for money, and moreover to ensure that the people for whom international aid is intended receive the best value from the money spent, a Conservative government would end the practice of simply giving aid money to countries in lump sums in return only for promises of action. Mitchell explains: 'We will link aid directly to independently audited evidence of real progress on the ground. Increasingly, we will pay "cash on delivery": giving an agreed amount to a recipient government for every extra child they get into school or every extra person who receives decent healthcare.' A Conservative government would also reduce or completely stop contributions to organisations like the UN Development Programme if they fail to deliver.

Perhaps the Conservative Party's most radical commitment in this arena, though, is its promise to create a 'MyAid Fund'. The fund, which would amount to £40 million, would be controlled directly by the public. As the party explains in the above policy paper: 'Individual British people will be able to vote on where and how to spend aid money. This will increase public understanding of, interest in and support for Britain's aid programme.'

Finally, the Conservative Party isn't a party that believes government has all the answers. It's a party that believes in the power of individuals to change their own lives. And for that reason a Conservative government wouldn't rely on aid alone to address the problems affecting the world's poorest countries. As Andrew Mitchell said in that same 2009 speech: 'We know that development is about much more than just aid. The single most important exit from grinding poverty is economic growth and trade. So we will re-emphasise the importance of private sector-led growth and wealth creation as the only path to prosperity.'

That will mean working with poorer countries to improve what the Conservatives have described as 'the building blocks of development', such as property rights, removing impediments to starting up a new business, the rule of law, infrastructure and so on. And it will also mean working internationally, principally through the EU, to ensure that barriers to trade with developing countries are removed. As the Western experience has proven, capitalism is the surest way to raise living standards and deliver a free and fair society. A Conservative government would work tirelessly to help those countries most in need to take advantage of all that the free market has to offer.

Under a Conservative government the reputation of international aid as little more than a limousine fund for dictators will come to an end. More money will be spent, yes, but far greater results will be achieved. And that benefits not just those in receipt of our aid, but also the UK itself.

Civil liberties

The United Kingdom has a proud history concerning civil liberties; indeed the very concept can be traced back to Magna Carta of 1215. But that proud history is being tarnished by the rise of the surveillance state under Labour. As the former Information Commissioner, Richard Thomas, warned in 2006:

> Today I fear we are in fact waking up to a surveillance society . . . As ever more information is collected, shared and used, it intrudes into our private space and leads to decisions which directly influence people's lives. Mistakes can also easily be made with serious consequences – false matches and other cases of mistaken identity, inaccurate facts or inferences, suspicions taken as reality, and breaches of security.

And, in 2007, as if to demonstrate the veracity of Thomas's fears, Privacy International, an NGO which monitors international privacy issues, ranked Britain forty-third out of forty-seven countries surveyed in terms of privacy protections. As the Conservative Party pointed out in its policy paper *Reversing the Rise of the Surveillance State*, this result was only slightly better than that achieved by Russia and China.

In 2009 David Cameron ably summarised the scale and ferocity of the attack which Labour have led on our civil liberties:

> The last twelve years of Labour government have diminished personal freedom and diluted political accountability . . . Today we are in danger of living in a control state. Almost a million innocent citizens are

caught in the web of the biggest DNA database in the world – larger than that of any dictatorship. Hundreds of shadowy powers allow officials to force their way past your front door . . . Every month over 1,000 surveillance operations are carried out, not just by law enforcement agencies but by other public bodies like councils and quangos. And the tentacles of the state can even rifle through your bins for juicy information.

For those who cherish our hard-won civil liberties and who understand the importance of ensuring that the state acts as servant and not as master, the case for reversing this rise is all too clear. And for those individuals, as will be seen below, the Conservative Party is the only party which guarantees that such an objective will be pursued as a matter of priority in government. But there are others who wonder what all the fuss is about, who maintain that if you have nothing to hide then you have nothing to fear. Yet, as Labour have demonstrated time and time again, there is plenty to fear. A few examples will serve to make this point.

In 2006 we learned that some 2,700 individuals had falsely been labelled criminals as a result of checks run though the Criminal Records Bureau. In 2007, the addresses, telephone numbers, religion and sexual orientation of hundreds of junior doctors were made openly available online after an error on an NHS website. Then, later in the year, we learned that HMRC had lost the records of twenty-five million people – which included everything from names to dates of birth to bank account details. Then, a month later, the DVLA admitted losing a hard drive containing the personal details of more than three million learner drivers. And one month after that, in January 2008, the MoD admitted losing a laptop which contained the personal details of 600,000 service personnel and individuals who had expressed interest in joining the armed forces.

As the Conservatives point out in *Reversing the Rise of the*

Surveillance State, Gordon Brown's response to failures such as these was astonishing: 'We can't promise that every single item of information will always be safe.'

So, whether you take a principled stand in defence of civil liberties or a practical stand in defence of your own personal information, it is clear that the surveillance state needs to be rolled back.

Under a Conservative government, action to dismantle the surveillance state would be swift. First and foremost, the Conservative Party has committed to reducing the number of large centralised databases and reducing the amount of personal details which are recorded by government (and to ensuring that where details are recorded, they are held only by specific authorities on a need-to-know basis).

The Conservatives have, for example, committed to scrapping the National Identity Register and the associated identity cards that Labour are so keen on. When it comes to ID cards (which, incidentally, would contain fifty pieces of personal information on the holder), the advantages of the system have yet to be established. As the Conservatives explain in the aforementioned policy paper, 'one by one, each grandiose claim for ID cards has crumbled'. Indeed, even the former Minister of State for Security, Counter-terrorism, Crime and Policing, Tony McNulty MP, eventually admitted that ID cards weren't the silver bullet Labour presented them to be: 'Perhaps in the past the government, in its enthusiasm, oversold the advantages of identity cards.' And as for the National Identity Register, its utility, if such can be said to exist, does not outweigh the inherent risk of storing such large volumes of personal information in one place.

And as for information being held on a strictly need-to-know basis, the National DNA Database is a case in point for how far things have gone in the wrong direction. At this very moment the DNA of one million completely innocent people is being held indefinitely and without justification on the database. This is nothing short of a national disgrace. A Conservative government would end this practice. In *Reversing the Rise of the Surveillance State* the party explains: 'DNA should be retained only whilst a person remains subject to investigation or until criminal proceedings have concluded.' Naturally, there would be a limited exception 'for those charged with certain crimes of violence and serious sexual offences'. But even then, the DNA would be retained for no longer than five years.

Secondly, the Conservatives would 'restrict and restrain council access to personal communications data'. Time and time again we hear about local councils using surveillance powers, intended to assist in the fight against terrorism, inappropriately. From the family in Dorset who were followed for a number of weeks to see if they lived in their children's school catchment area, to Broadland District Council's use of a plane equipped with a thermal imaging camera to identify residents wasting too much energy, the need to rein councils in is all too clear. A Conservative government would reform the Regulation of Investigative Powers Act 2000, which extended surveillance power to councils, restricting them to accessing communications data only 'for the purposes of assisting investigation into serious crime'. And to ensure democratic accountability, only the council leader would be able to authorise such action.

Thirdly, a Conservative government would strengthen the power of the Information Commissioner to hold the government to account. For example, the commissioner would be granted the power to carry out ad hoc inspections of government departments on their management of data. Crucially, where departments fell short of the mark the commissioner would be able to impose fines.

Fourthly, the Conservative Party has committed to ensuring that in the future when the government wants to create new data-sharing powers – for example between government departments, quangos etc – it will have to do so by creating new primary legislation, rather than simply by order of the secretary of state (as Labour have previously attempted to do). The temptation on the part of governments to grab new power has to be restricted; the Conservative Party would ensure that it is.

Finally, the Conservatives would make one minister and one senior civil servant within each government department responsible for data security, although, naturally, the ultimate responsibility would rest with the minister. Without this kind of individual responsibility the incentive will always exist for politicians to pass the buck – as we saw when Labour blamed a junior civil servant for the HMRC data loss outlined above.

Civil liberties form the very foundation of our society. If we don't vigorously protect them we will lose more than just our personal information, we'll lose our way of life. A Conservative government would be as unrelenting in attacking the surveillance state and all the dangers that come with it as Labour are in placing the perceived interests of the state above the very real interests of individuals.

The family

To say that the Conservative Party under David Cameron is big on family would be an understatement on a par with saying Roger Federer is a pretty decent tennis player. For the Conservatives, family isn't simply a priority; it is perhaps *the* priority (at least in terms of domestic policy). From dealing with crime, to improving education, to anti-social behaviour, to the United Kingdom's ability to compete on a world stage with emerging economies like China, the Conservative Party sees the family unit as the foundation upon which a better society can be built. As David Cameron puts it:

> Britain has one of the highest rates of family breakdown in Europe. And we also have some of the worst social problems. That is why I say it is time for change to make this country more family friendly so we can turn around the social breakdown, turn around the crime and anti-social behaviour, turn around this unacceptable situation where our cost of living is going up and the quality of life is going down.

In sum, it is a central tenet of the Conservative Party's philosophy that many, if not most of the nation's problems can be attributed to family breakdown, and that by strengthening families the Conservative Party can strengthen society. But for the Conservative Party it isn't just about supporting and strengthening the traditional nuclear family with 2.4 children, it's about supporting all stable and loving families, whether single parent, divorced parents, gay couples with children or widows or widowers bringing up children.

Getting the finances right: removing Labour's disincentives

But in supporting all stable and loving families there are some startling facts that cannot be brushed under the carpet. As highlighted by the Centre for Social Justice, a child whose parents have split up is 75 per cent more likely to suffer educational failure, 70 per cent more likely to become addicted to drugs, 50 per cent more likely to become an alcoholic, 40 per cent more likely to get into serious debt, and 35 per cent more likely to become welfare dependent or experience unemployment. But despite this, the Labour government has actually contrived a benefits system that discourages couples from living together. As the *Repair Plan for Social Reform* illustrates:

A study by [the Labour MP] Frank Field found that two-parent households need a far greater income than a lone parent to move past the poverty line. He found that two parents with two children had to earn £240 a week to have a net income of £295 and lift themselves above the poverty line. By contrast, a lone parent with the same number of children needed to earn just £76 a week to gain a net income of £230, £5 above the poverty line. Because the government's policies discriminate so heavily against families with two parents, it is harder for couple families to escape poverty. As a result the risk of poverty for children in two-parent families actually rose in 2006 from 21 per cent to 23 per cent. In addition, 60 per cent of poor children live in couple families.

It's hardly surprising then that the respected and independent Institute for Fiscal Studies discovered that there are over 200,000 more single parents claiming tax credits in the UK than actually exist according to the government's own figures. And if we know anything about government figures after the last twelve years it's that they're nothing if not optimistic. Clearly, the need for change is overwhelming.

Our response to this is very simple: under a Conservative government the disincentive to cohabitation in the tax credits system would end. As outlined in the *Repair Plan* the Conservatives would 'increase the Working Tax Credit that couples currently receive from £3,570 to £5,604, an increase of up to £39 per week'. That would mean just under two million of the poorest couples with children receiving an average of £32 a week extra. Incredibly, this would result in almost a third of a million children in two-parent families being lifted out of poverty. With this one simple change, the incentive for couples with children to live apart would disappear.

Labour's penalties against couples don't end there. The UK is one of the few countries in the developed world in which marriage is not recognised in the tax system. Despite making a public and

solemn commitment to one another, married couples do not enjoy
any acknowledgement from the state in the form of tax incentives.
The Conservative Party would give marriage and civil partnerships the support in the tax system they deserve, as David Willetts,
shadow Minister for Universities and Skills, outlined during his 2009
Conservative Party conference speech:

> Some countries do treat us just as individuals for income tax purposes.
> That is what they do in Turkey; oh yes, and in Mexico too. Labour
> may believe in the Turkish–Mexican model, but most other advanced
> Western countries do recognise marriage in the income tax system.
> That's what they do in France. That's what they do in Germany. That's
> what they do in the USA. And that's what we'll do too.

Labour's financial war against families isn't restricted to couples,
though. For example, as David Cameron highlighted in his 2009
Conservative Party conference speech: 'In Gordon Brown's Britain
if you're a single mother with two kids earning £150 a week the
withdrawal of benefits and the additional taxes mean that for every
extra pound you earn, you keep just four pence.' By any measure,
this is a disgrace.

This shocking state of affairs isn't just anti-family, it's anti-
common sense and it's nothing short of morally reprehensible. The
Conservative Party under David Cameron is committed to removing these kinds of disincentive from the tax and benefits system.

Helping couples stay together

Moving beyond finances, the Conservative Party recognises the
need for relationships to be nurtured if they are to survive all that
life throws at them. And that means utilising relationship support.
With this in mind the Conservatives have pledged to ensure
'proper funding for organisations delivering relationship support',

to provide more help to ensure those organisations can recruit the people needed to deliver that support, and to 'de-stigmatising the whole area of relationship support'. Perhaps most importantly of all, though, the Conservatives believe that public sector employees should have a duty to direct families toward the 'necessary support that exists in the voluntary and private sector'. Crucially, the extra cost to the taxpayer of such direction on the part of individuals like registrars, GPs and health visitors is nil.

In striving to help couples stay together, there are two facts that act as a driving force behind Conservative policy in this area:

1. Parents are more likely to separate during the year after the birth of their child than at any other time;
2. The early years in a child's development are critically important in determining how they will perform at school, as well as their long-term psychological and emotional development.

Taken together, these facts mean one thing: early intervention is key.

Central to the Conservative Party's approach of early intervention, as described in the *Repair Plan*, is the introduction of 'a genuinely universal health visiting service across the country so that every family has the support and advice they need to give their children a good start in life'. Astonishingly, though, despite the overwhelming case for a comprehensive health visiting service, Labour have actually reduced the number of health visitors by over 2,000 since 2004. However, to make their vision a reality, the Conservatives would ensure that:

1. 4,200 new health visitors are recruited across the UK;
2. In the later weeks of pregnancy, mothers would receive a minimum of two visits from a health visitor in their own home. These visits would focus on providing advice on issues such as nutrition for the mother and child-raising;

3. During the first two weeks after the birth of a child, families would receive a minimum of six hours of assistance from a health visitor in the home;

4. For the following six months of a child's life, families will receive one visit every two weeks from a health visitor;

5. During the second six months of a child's life, families would receive monthly visits from a health visitor, focusing on providing advice and support on issues such as establishing good sleeping patterns and transitioning to solid foods;

6. Between the ages of one and five, families would receive a minimum of two visits a year from a health visitor, focusing on providing advice and support on issues such as hearing and vision tests and immunisation.

Finally, the Conservatives would create a £10 million Child Health Inequalities Fund to provide additional support to the poorest families in society. In order to pay for this universal service we would use the funds allocated by the Labour government to create a new batch of 'outreach workers' for Sure Start. As the Conservatives point out, those 'outreach workers' 'lack the professional training of health visitors (and will therefore be less likely according to survey evidence to command the confidence of parents)'.

Ensuring a healthy work/life balance

The time parents get to spend with their children in the first year of their children's lives is as precious as it is critically important. But despite the Labour government increasing paid maternity leave to fifty-two weeks it is clear that significant weaknesses exist in the system. The Conservative Party would maintain the guarantee to fifty-two weeks' paid leave but would introduce a scheme called Flexible Parental Leave (FPL) which would allow parents to share the time between them. The first fourteen weeks of leave would automatically apply to the mother to enable her, as the Conservative Party puts it, 'to recover from the effects of childbirth' and to ensure that she is able to form a strong bond with her child. As for the remaining thirty-eight weeks, the Conservative Party explains, 'the mother could take off the whole fifty-two weeks; the father could take over FPL at any time during the final thirty-eight weeks; or the mother and father could simultaneously take off up to twenty-six weeks each . . . Parents who simultaneously take FPL would be eligible for double the rate of statutory maternity pay during the period of concurrent leave.' As mentioned above, though, the Conservative Party's view of a loving and stable family isn't restricted to the traditional nuclear family with 2.4 children; accordingly, the mother's partner in a same-sex relationship would enjoy the same rights.

But clearly, the first year of a child's life is only the start. And when it comes to the subsequent years of a child's life, the Conservatives have big plans. As we explain, we want to 'make flexible working available to as many people as possible'. A first step in this will be ensuring that the UK's largest employer, the public sector, 'becomes a world leader in providing flexible working opportunities'. But on top of this, the Conservative Party recognises the role the private sector has to play and would accordingly 'extend the right to request flexible working to every parent with a child under the age of eighteen'.

When the worst happens

It is abundantly clear that radical reform is needed in the care system. In his 2009 Conservative Party conference speech, David Willetts laid down the brutal facts: '23,000 children are taken into care every year. But the state is a very bad parent. One in four teenage girls leaving care are mothers or mothers-to-be within a year. People who have been in care make up less than one in a hundred of the population but they are a third of the people in prison. This is a national scandal.'

Unsurprisingly, this is an area the Conservative Party would be looking at very closely when in government because, as Willetts pointed out in the same speech, 'it must not be like this. We can do better.'

Furthermore, the Conservatives have committed to ensuring that when children lose their parents, family and friends, particularly grandparents, will have a legal right to be their guardians. The present situation, where the vast majority of children are thrust upon strangers regardless of the willingness of family to take them in, simply isn't right.

A diverse society and
social cohesion

It goes without saying that a strong society is built upon strong communities, with a shared identity, common values and mutual respect. One need only consider the history of Northern Ireland to comprehend the tragedy which inevitably consumes a society composed of divided communities. And yet, when one considers the modern United Kingdom it's clear that our communities are becoming increasingly divided. Indeed, as the chairman of the Equality and Human Rights Commission, Trevor Phillips, warned in 2005, there is a danger that as a society we are 'sleepwalking into segregation'.

That we have found ourselves in this situation is hardly surprising given, as the Conservatives have described it, Labour's 'state-driven multiculturalism'. As the shadow Justice Minister, Dominic Grieve

MP, pointed out in March 2009, the UK has endured 'a decade of ranking people as members of neatly categorised ethnic, religious or social groups, rather than treating everyone as an individual in their own right'.

This determination to define people as distinct groups rather than as members of a wider British community has only been reinforced by Labour's attempt to do all it can to suppress any notion of a British identity. Is it any wonder that many of the communities which make up modern Britain find it difficult to identify with British values when the government has opted to discourage the teaching of British history for fear it might offend, and as Grieve pointed out in the same speech as above, has encouraged young people to be 'contemptuous of people who in the past did not live up to the then unknown values of modern Britain'? Is it any wonder that immigrants to the UK have a tough time developing a sense of belonging when, as the shadow Minister for Community Cohesion and Social Action Baroness Warsi, has pointed out, rather than encourage people to speak English, Labour have preferred instead that documents be translated into multiple languages?

Whether through failing to adequately criticise practices which fundamentally offend the British way of life – such as forced marriage – out of some misguided sense of cultural sensitivity, or through the creation of a culture in the public sector which feels it's right to ban hot cross buns in case they offend non-Christians, it is clear that for all Labour's talk of 'multiculturalism' all they have done is, in Baroness Warsi's words, '[to force] Britain's diverse communities to still define themselves as different, patronisingly special and tempting them to compete against each other for public funds'.

And on top of all of this, Labour have failed to address the issue of immigration. Between 1993 and 1997 average net immigration each year was 51,000, but between 2004 and 2008 it had risen to

209,000. Not only has this unchecked immigration put extra strain on Britain's public services, it has also played into the hands of extreme political groups like the BNP who have used it to further undermine community cohesion.

If Britain is to enjoy the kind of strong community cohesion which befits its status as a tolerant liberal democracy, and which is necessary for it to flourish in the twenty-first century, the era of 'state-driven multiculturalism' has to come to an end. Only the Conservative Party are committed to seeing that objective achieved.

Building social cohesion

Under a Conservative government the days of pigeonholing people into specific groups would come to an end. For example, when it comes to providing support for community groups, a Conservative government would make decisions based entirely on the results achieved by those groups (for example in alleviating poverty) rather than on the basis of ethnicity or faith. On top of this, a Conservative government would also devolve more power to local authorities, who, as the Conservative Party points out on its website, 'are better placed to make decisions for their communities'. Big government has to be broken down if communities are to thrive.

Additionally, a Conservative government would not shy away from promoting British values. On a practical level this would mean, for example, ensuring greater emphasis on the teaching of British history in school. Not only would this ensure that the settled population is familiar with the evolution of British values such as pluralism and tolerance, but it would also provide more recent immigrants with a much greater opportunity to find a common identity with their new home. But promoting British values also means, at times, being clear about what values and practices we aren't prepared to tolerate as a nation. With that in mind, a Conservative government would vigorously tackle practices like forced marriage and female genital mutilation.

The Conservative Party has also pledged to offer English language courses to all those who don't currently speak English. As the party has made clear, in government it would ensure that the English language is cemented 'as the bedrock of our national identity'.

Crucially, though, the Conservative Party hasn't been afraid to point out that community cohesion isn't something that a government can deliver by itself. Rather, as it makes clear on its website: 'everyone must do all they can to make this a fairer and more just society – helping others, creating opportunity, and ensuring that no one is excluded'.

Immigration

As indicated above, unchecked immigration has done tremendous damage to social cohesion, and that's to say nothing of the strain it has placed on public services. Accordingly, the Conservative Party has committed to a twofold strategy with regard to immigration:

1. Placing reasonable controls on immigration;
2. Properly policing Britain's borders.

Firstly, with regard to economic migrants from outside the EU, a Conservative government would change immigration eligibility requirements so that only those individuals who would provide an economic benefit to the UK could enter. On top of this, the Conservatives have also committed to setting an annual limit on the number of non-EU economic migrants who can enter the UK. This limit would vary from year to year and would depend, for example, on prevailing economic circumstances.

Secondly, in order to fight illegal immigration a Conservative government would create a UK Border Police Force; something which is desperately overdue. The party's website explains:

Unlike Labour's Border Agency, which does not even include the police, our force will have the power to stop, search, detain and prosecute the terrorists, traffickers and illegal immigrants who currently slip through the net. Only then will we be able to start making Britain safer.

Immigration is vitally important to the UK economy. But only by controlling it can we protect public services and reinforce social cohesion.

Crime

The UK faces a crime crisis. The stories of human tragedy are all too frequent. Fiona Pilkington killed herself and her mentally disabled daughter by setting fire to their car after suffering ten years of unimaginable abuse at the hands of local yobs. Sophie Lancaster was kicked to death by a gang of youths because she dressed like a goth. Sukhwinder Singh was stabbed to death after he tried to retrieve a young woman's handbag from thieves. The list goes on and on. And much though we might like to delude ourselves that these are isolated incidents and unrepresentative of the level of crime in the UK, we need only look at the crime statistics to see that they are merely the tip of the iceberg. To take only a small sample, in the previous twelve years:

- Violent crime has almost doubled;
- Gun violence has gone up fourfold;
- Stabbings leading to death have gone up by a full quarter.

As the Conservative Party has rightly observed, fatal violence like that in the examples above can strike absolutely anyone at absolutely any time. This has to stop.

Labour declared that they were going to be 'tough on crime, and tough on the causes of crime'. But their response has fallen far short of this commitment. Rather than tackle crime effectively, Labour engaged in a futile effort to simply legislate it away, creating over 3,000 new crimes since 1997. As the figures above demonstrate, though, this response was at best misguided and at worst recklessly irresponsible.

Getting to the heart of the problem

The root causes of crime are many and varied. But one which stands out as a priority is alcohol. The shadow Home Secretary, Chris Grayling MP, was uncompromising in his 2009 Conservative Party conference speech:

> No one thinks that the government's 24-hour drinking regime has led to the creation of a 'continental café culture'. We're not talking about stopping people enjoying a few drinks in the pub. But things have gone far too far. Our town centres on a Friday and Saturday night can be battle zones for our police. Local parks and local estates are blighted by gangs of young troublemakers . . . fuelled by alcohol given to them by irresponsible adults. I have talked to people up and down the country whose lives are being ruined by antisocial behaviour. It's time we stood up for them.

But in standing up to those who engage in anti-social behaviour as a result of alcohol abuse, the Conservatives have always been clear that a path must be struck which deals with the troublemakers whilst respecting responsible drinkers. Accordingly, a Conservative government would take the following steps to address the binge drinking culture that does so much to contribute to crime in the UK.

Firstly, it is abundantly clear that alcohol is available far too cheaply, and cheap alcohol only serves to encourage the problem drinker. A classic example, one highlighted by Grayling in the same speech, is the group of underage drinkers taking advantage of super-cheap and super-strength beers and ciders. To address this problem, the Conservatives have pledged to increase the price of a four-pack of super-strength beer by £1.33 and 'to more than double the tax on super-strength cider'. Alcopops will be targeted too, with the Conservatives insuring that the price of a large bottle goes up by a full £1.50. As Grayling explains, though, 'these taxes will not hit responsible drinkers. The ordinary pint in the pub will not be affected and there'll be exemptions for some local traditional products.'

As we all know, larger supermarkets often sell alcohol at a loss in order to draw people in and encourage them to buy other goods. It stands to reason, then, that such supermarkets might be minded to swallow the cost of the above alcohol price increases and continue to sell at a loss. The Conservatives won't stand for this practice. Under a Conservative government, supermarkets would be banned from doing this. The days of below-cost alcohol will be over.

Additionally, a Conservative government would empower people to control the number of venues which are licensed to sell alcohol in their area by giving communities the right to veto applications for new licences. Councils would additionally be able to curtail opening hours, and any venues contravening these hours would be hit with harsh penalties.

As for underage drinking, the Conservatives would operate a three-strikes rule. Any venues that sold alcohol to people under the age of eighteen would on the first occasion be met with higher fines than have ever previously existed. If they sold to underage drinkers again they would be closed down for a number of days. And, if they were still not deterred and continued to sell to underage drinkers they would have their licences removed permanently.

Empowering the police

Unsurprisingly, effective policing sits at the heart of the Conservative strategy to address crime. Lessons from abroad, for example New York, have demonstrated that to reduce incidences of more serious violent crime, police have to deal with minor incidences of crime. A Conservative government will see that this approach is brought to bear on criminality in the UK.

But for the police to get on with the job of policing they must have the handcuffs of bureaucracy taken off their wrists. Two great examples of this are Stop and Account forms and Stop and Search forms. As the Conservatives' *Repair Plan for Social Reform* explains, Stop and Account forms were introduced to build confidence amongst ethnic minority communities by keeping a record of stops carried out by the police. The noble intent of the form is to be applauded, but the practical impact is deeply troubling. The form comprises a total of forty questions, is one foot long and, according to the Home Office's own statistics, an average police officer will fill one out for every 2.2 hours he or she is on duty outside the police station. As highlighted in the above policy paper, this equates to an incredible 778,571 police hours per year. Over three-quarters of a million frontline police hours on admin is not time well spent. Similarly, filling out Stop and Search forms takes up an astonishing 397,964 frontline police hours. The Conservatives would scrap both these forms. To ensure public confidence, police officers would instead radio in the basic details of any search carried out, and this would be recorded at the station.

Whilst freeing up more police hours by reducing the administrative burden associated with stops and searches, the Conservative Party would also give the police a freer hand in carrying out stops and searches in specific circumstances. As the above policy paper outlines: 'We propose to empower police sergeants to authorise stop and search of pedestrians and vehicles in a specific area for a period of up to six hours, if they reasonably believe that a serious crime has occurred or is about to occur. This would include stop and search for offensive weapons and drugs.' Moreover, this could be extended to a maximum stop and search period of forty-eight hours if an officer of superintendent rank or higher deemed it appropriate.

The empowerment of police sergeants would not end there. The Conservative Party would give custody sergeants the power to decide whether or not to charge an individual for all offences tried in a magistrates' court. By doing this the Conservatives estimate that up to one million hours of police time could be saved, as police would no longer have their time taken up by preparing paperwork for the Crown Prosecution Service. Labour took this power away from the police and ended up costing the public desperately needed man-hours; a Conservative government will give that power, and that time, back.

Another innovative approach being taken by the Conservatives is in the use of 'virtual courts' to reduce the amount of police time being taken up by travelling to and from magistrates' courts. This system essentially works by creating a video link between the police station's custody suite and the magistrates' court. As pointed out by the *Repair Plan for Social Reform*, when trialled by the Metropolitan Police the results were nothing short of astonishing: 'In the trials the average time for bail cases was nine and a half days and custody cases half a day without virtual courts. Both of these were reduced to less than three and a half hours with the introduction of virtual courts.' The figures speak for themselves, and the Conservatives are committed to seeing virtual courts rolled out across police forces.

Tackling knife crime

Dealing with knife crime is a key priority for the Conservatives. The list of people, young and old, who have died as a result of knife crime is as horrifying as it is long. We have already outlined above the power which will be extended to the police to authorise stops and searches in given area for up to forty-eight hours. But this is only one aspect of the Conservative approach.

On top of this the Conservatives have committed to employing mobile knife scanners on public transport and on the pavements. Boris Johnson has been utilising just such a scheme in London to great effect, and a Conservative government would see it rolled out across the UK. Additionally, they would ensure that 'anyone carrying a knife without a reasonable excuse should expect to be prosecuted'. Incredibly, as the Conservatives have revealed, under Labour over a third of people carrying knives 'have been let off with a caution or final warning'. Most importantly, though, anyone convicted of carrying a knife could expect to receive a custodial sentence under a Conservative government.

Empowering the public

One of the most tragic side effects of Labour's approach to crime has been the growing culture of 'walking on by'. According to the Reform think tank, people in Britain are less likely to intervene to stop a crime than in many of our closest neighbours, such as Germany. And it's hardly surprising. Far too often innocent people find themselves prosecuted for intervening. If we are to become a society that isn't afraid to intervene, this sorry situation has to change. And the Conservative Party will see that that change is made. One example of this is self-defence in the home.

It is a sad indictment of our society that when an innocent person's home is broken into, they can't be sure that they won't face prosecution for defending themselves and their family. So bad is the situation that even threatening a would-be burglar can result in a warning from the police, as Myleene Klass found out. At the moment, the law allows people to use 'reasonable force' to defend themselves. But, as Chris Grayling has said: 'What we need to do is make sure the courts recognise there is a higher bar to jump before we send a householder to prison.' With that in mind a Conservative government would change the law so that people would only be prosecuted if their action was 'grossly disproportionate'. With that one change the ambiguity in the law would disappear and house-holders would be able to act decisively and without fear when the worst happens. The law must favour the victim and not the criminal, and the Conservatives would see that that is the case.

The policy that most stands out, though, in the Conservative Party's arsenal to combat crime is the commitment to creating elected police commissioners. The rationale for this is very simple, according to the *Repair Plan for Social Reform*: 'Instead of being directed by, and accountable to, the Home Secretary, police forces should be directed by and accountable to the communities they serve.' Such police commissioners would have wide-ranging respon-sibilities, including setting the police budget; hiring and firing the chief constable; setting local policing priorities; monitoring how well the police perform against local targets and ensuring best value from the local police budget; and ensuring 'beat meetings' are held in each neighbourhood on a quarterly basis, so that the public can hold the police to account for their performance.

By giving local people the power to elect a police commissioner, the Conservatives will give them the power to shape the direction and nature of policing in their area. Labour's centralised targets will be replaced in favour of a local populace with the power to set their own priorities.

But the power to elect a police commissioner isn't enough if people don't have access to adequate information about the effect of local policing. That means providing the public with access to robust data on crime. As the Conservatives have explained: 'At the moment at the police force level . . . only the total number of recorded offences in each of the nine categories is available online

– sub-categories are not.' Clearly, if people are to be able to hold the police to account through their elected commissioner, they need access to much more detailed information. A Conservative government would require all police forces to 'publish their local crime statistics online on a monthly basis and, separately, in map form'. The crime map for each police force area would detail occurrences of 'a large number of offences' right down to the street level. Naturally the maps would be sensitive to the needs of victims and wouldn't, for example, list which specific houses were burgled.

A Conservative government would put power in the hands of the people, enable them to hold their police force to account, ensure that the hands of the police have the ties of Labour bureaucracy removed, address the root causes of crime (such as binge drinking) and, ultimately, deliver a United Kingdom that starts to see the kind of reductions in crime enjoyed by New York City when it finally got to grips with the problem.

Parliamentary and constitutional reform

It's no secret that the Conservative Party has been critical of what it calls Labour's 'constitutional vandalism'. And vandalism it certainly is. From their botched House of Lords reform – which has left the Upper House in a state of limbo – to their successful efforts to undermine the right to trial by jury in criminal matters, Labour's love-affair with the notion of constitutional reform has proven tremendously damaging. What's more, just as Labour have paid scant regard to the British constitution, so too have they attempted to undermine at every turn the ability of Parliament to hold the government to account. The Conservative Party is committed to putting things right.

House of Lords reform

When it comes to constitutional reform, the issue that most often springs to mind is the House of Lords. And for good reason. At first, in their 1997 election manifesto, Labour promised to end the right of hereditary peers to sit in the Second Chamber, but when elected they reneged on this pledge, removing some hereditaries, but not all. Then in their 2001 manifesto they promised to move onto the next stage of Lords reform (having not followed through on the first) and made clear they would 'allow a free vote on the composition of the House'. Now, nine years and one (soon to be two) manifestos on, the House of Lords continues to exist in the halfway house created on the back of the 1997 manifesto. This mess needs to be sorted out once and for all. The Conservative Party has committed to delivering a substantially elected Second Chamber and to reducing the number of Lords who sit in the House. However, to ensure that this is done properly the Conservatives won't simply rush headfirst into reform in the way Labour has. Instead, a decision on the final composition of the house will be reached through consultation and ultimately consensus.

Strengthening Parliament

Under Labour, Parliament has become little more than a rubber-stamping operation for the government's agenda. The most memorable example of Labour's contempt for Parliament came in the aftermath of the suggestion from the Modernisation Committee, chaired by the late Robin Cook, that select committee chairs should no longer be chosen by party whips and that they should be paid an additional stipend. Labour rejected the idea that whips should have this power stripped from them, but gave its approval to the creation of an additional stipend, thus boosting the patronage of the whips even further and ensuring that scrutiny remained weak!

Unlike Labour, the Conservative Party isn't afraid of scrutiny and believes that governments must be held properly to account by Parliament. Accordingly, a Conservative government would end the practice of whips choosing select committee chairs and would instead have them elected by backbench MPs. On top of this the Conservatives have committed to removing the government's total control over business in the House of Commons by giving the Commons itself more power over what goes on (this would include Opposition Day debates, private members' bills and the like). Additionally, when bills reach the committee stage, a Conservative government would give MPs a free vote.

But perhaps the biggest sign of the deep respect the Conservative Party has for Parliament is its pledge to ensure that in future, governments will have to get its approval before deploying British troops into combat overseas.

Whereas Labour have done everything they could to weaken the power of Parliament, the Conservatives understand the need for government to be effectively held to account.

Strengthening democracy

Just as it is committed to strengthening Parliament, so too is the Conservative Party committed to strengthening democracy more generally. For example, the Electoral Commission and the Committee on Standards in Public Life have been warning for years that the current system of household voter registration (under which one person in a household is responsible for the electoral registration of everyone in that household) is seriously open to abuse. In recognition of this the Conservative Party has promised to implement a system of individual voter registration as a matter of priority. What's more, the Conservatives have guaranteed never to use a system of all-postal voting such as Labour employed during the 2004 local elections (against the strong advice of the Electoral Commission).

Perhaps the Conservatives' most important commitment vis-à-vis strengthening democracy is their pledge to do away with the absurd system whereby the size of parliamentary constituencies, in terms of the number of voters, varies massively across the UK. It is only right that the vote of any UK citizen should have the same weight regardless of where they live. Accordingly, a Conservative government would ask the Boundary Commission to ensure that all constituencies are roughly the same size. On top of this, the Conservatives have also pledged to reduce the number of MPs by 10 per cent (for more on this see the chapter on Restoring Trust and Honesty in Politics).

Strengthening engagement

Two final commitments by the Conservatives that will bring change to Parliament shouldn't pass without notice. First, the Conservatives have pledged to introduce a new system of petitions. Unlike the Downing Street petitions delivered by Gordon Brown, which hold no power, the Conservatives would ensure that any petition submitted to Parliament with the signatures of 100,000 voters would result in a formal debate on the topic in question. Second, and most significantly, a Conservative government would introduce a 'public reading stage' directly after a bill's second reading in the Commons. During this stage the bill would be placed online and members of the public would be able to make detailed comments on the various aspects of the bill in question.

Scotland, Wales and Northern Ireland

The Conservative Party is above all else a unionist party. The simple truth therefore is this: if you don't believe in the inherent value of the United Kingdom as a nation comprising England, Scotland, Wales and Northern Ireland then the Conservative Party simply isn't for you. But if the continuing union of these four parts of the United Kingdom is important to you, then the Conservative Party under David Cameron is the only party that has your interests genuinely at heart.

However, whilst the Conservatives are unflinching in their support for the union, it should not pass without notice that they are equally committed to devolution. Devolving power to people is a central tenet of modern Conservative Party philosophy, and the Scottish Parliament, Welsh Assembly and Northern Ireland Assembly have a critical role to play in ensuring that the decisions which affect people's lives are taken as closely to the people they affect as possible.

A corollary of the commitment to the Union is an understanding that each of the members of the Union enjoys its own unique characteristics, challenges and aspirations. Unsurprisingly, these differences are reflected in the Conservative Party's approach to each country.

Scotland

For those who value the Union it is clear that the greatest threat to its future is the Scottish National Party. Their fight for independence has ramifications that extend far beyond the borders of Scotland; first and foremost, if Scotland were to become independent it would raise serious questions about the continuing future of the union between the remaining members of the United Kingdom. Accordingly, the front line in the Conservative Party's battle to protect the union is in Scotland.

Crucially though, the Conservative fight to maintain Scotland's place in the union stands in stark opposition to Labour's scare-mongering that Scotland would be economically weak if it left the UK. As David Cameron has said himself, 'it would be wrong to suggest that Scotland could not be another . . . successful, independent country.' Instead the Conservatives would appeal both to the heart and to the head, highlighting the enormous practical benefits that Scots derive from the union, whilst also explaining what would be lost 'politically, culturally and historically' if Scotland were to split from the rest of the UK. For those who want to ensure that Scotland continues to be a member of the UK, the Conservative Party is the only party offering a positive vision for the future of the union and the only party that is committed to fight to its last breath for the union.

On the English side of the border, one significant point of tension in the relationship between Scotland and England has been the ability of MPs representing Scottish constituencies to vote on legislation that affects only England, whilst both they and MPs representing English constituencies are prevented from voting on matters which fall within the power of the Scottish Parliament. To address this problem, Cameron has committed to ensuring that in future MPs representing English constituencies be given a decisive say on legislation affecting only England. This is the only practical solution to the 'West Lothian Question' offered by any of the parties.

In December 2009, Alex Salmond admitted that he had not met with Gordon Brown in almost a year. Despite the worst recession the United Kingdom has ever faced, despite shocking levels of unemployment, despite the loss of so many of the small businesses which together form the backbone of Scotland's economy, the Prime Minister and the First Minister couldn't find the time to meet one another. This incredible state of affairs only serves to reinforce the extent to which the relationship between Westminster and Holyrood has broken down under Brown's tenure as Prime Minister. Cameron has committed to ensuring this absurd situation would not continue under a Conservative administration, explaining in an article for *Scotland on Sunday* that 'I would be a Prime Minister who would work constructively with any administration at Holyrood for the good of Scotland, and I would be in regular contact with the First Minister no matter which party he or she came from'. On top of this, Cameron has made clear that the Secretary of State for Scotland would be required to have monthly meetings with the First Minister, and that Cabinet members would be required to maintain regular contact with their counterparts in Scotland. What's more, in stark contrast to Labour's refusal to allow ministers to appear before Scottish Parliament committees, Cameron would ensure that Conservative ministers remained open to all reasonable requests for such appearances.

Wales

The Conservative Party's commitment to Wales's place in the United Kingdom is every bit as strong as its commitment to Scotland. As Cheryl Gillan MP, shadow Secretary of State for Wales, has said: 'Wales brings so much to the table as a partner in the United Kingdom, with its breathtaking scenery in its National Parks and coastline, with its proud heritage, culture and language and with the talents, innovation and hard work of its people in industry and in the farming communities.' As such, the Conservative Party is committed to fighting Plaid Cymru's attempts to break the bonds of kinship between Wales and the rest of UK.

But whilst the Conservatives are steadfast in their desire to see Wales remain in the union, it's clear that a much more pressing problem for Wales in the immediate term is the extent to which its people have suffered under Labour. By any measure, Wales is a country in desperate need of change. Since 1997 council tax has almost doubled, in 2008 Wales had the third highest rate of violent crime in the world, it remains the poorest part of the UK and prosperity levels have fallen even further behind the UK average, unemployment is higher in Wales than in any other part of the UK (astonishingly, nearly half the total number of jobs lost in the UK in the final quarter of 2009 were in Wales – for the second quarter in a row); the list goes on and on.

The Conservative Party recognises the immense challenges facing Wales, just as it recognises those faced by the UK as a whole, and it is the only party with the policies and the dynamism to address the unique adversities facing the people of Wales and to put this great nation back on its feet.

Northern Ireland

The irony for Northern Ireland is that for all the fighting over its place in the union, its citizens were never truly able to make their voice heard at the top table. The politics of the province was dominated exclusively by small, local parties that only contested seats within the six counties. As William Hague explains: 'They can never form the government of the United Kingdom. And their MPs can never be ministers in a government of the United Kingdom.' From one general election to the next the votes of the people of Northern Ireland meant very little. They could choose to vote for no one at all, or vote for someone who would have no influence whatsoever over the vast areas of policy that had not been devolved: taxation, public spending, defence, foreign affairs and so on.

Thankfully, the Conservative Party has brought this travesty of so-called democracy to an end by entering into a partnership with the Ulster Unionist Party. Under the partnership the parties will field joint candidates under a Conservative and Unionist banner, all under a joint UK-wide manifesto, and any MPs elected under the partnership would take the Conservative whip. Hague explains: 'Any Conservative and Unionist MP elected here will take the Conservative whip and have the same rights and responsibilities as every other Conservative MP from England, Scotland and Wales. And that means being able to serve as a minister in a Conservative and Unionist government for the whole United Kingdom. That's a claim that no other party in Northern Ireland can make at the forthcoming election.' Under the partnership, though, the UUP would remain free to act as it wishes in the Northern Ireland Assembly without any interference from the Conservative Party, in recognition of the unique characteristics of the province.

One other peculiar feature of democracy in Northern Ireland is the practice of 'double jobbing' by elected representatives. Rather than opt to treat one elected position as their full-time job, they hold several posts (meaning that none get the full attention they deserve). Incredibly, there are some who are councillors, MLAs, MPs and ministers in the Northern Ireland Assembly all at the same time. The phrase 'jack of all trades, master of none' springs to mind. The Conservative Party would stop this practice; politicians would have to pick one job.

Restoring trust and honesty in politics

It's no secret that trust in Parliament and politicians is at an all-time low. From the 'dodgy dossier' on Iraq to the MPs' expenses scandal of 2009, the public have time and time again been given reason to doubt the honesty and integrity of their elected officials. Dealing with this crisis is a matter of fierce urgency: if we fail to act we run the risk of delivering serious and long-term damage to British parliamentary democracy. But whereas Labour have opted to sit back and hope for the best, the Conservative Party has a proactive plan for restoring trust and honesty in British politics.

No party escaped unscathed from the expenses scandal, and those who abused the system were rightly pulled through the mud. But when it came to taking action at the time, the Conservative Party under David Cameron moved first and moved farthest. As a signal of the Conservative Party's commitment to transparency and honesty with the British public, Cameron ordered that the expenses and second home allowances of all shadow Cabinet members be made available to the public online and in full, and that they be updated on a weekly basis. Moreover he immediately banned Conservative MPs from claiming for furniture, food and household goods and from engaging in the practice of 'flipping' second home designations. Furthermore, he created a Scrutiny Panel to investigate any excessive claims by Conservative MPs and empowered the panel to demand repayments where necessary. Whilst the other parties dithered, the Conservative Party took decisive action.

Of course, these were merely the actions that were within the power of the main opposition party to take. The Conservatives in government would go much further. Firstly, with regard to expenses in particular, they remain committed to ensuring that the proposals put forward by Sir Christopher Kelly in his report on expenses are implemented in full, ensuring a rigorous expenses system that provides MPs only with what they absolutely need – nothing more.

But addressing the problems inherent in the current expenses system will not, by itself, be enough to restore trust in Parliament and politics in general. With that in mind the Conservative Party has committed to cutting the number of MPs by 10 per cent. At the moment there are simply too many individuals on the green benches; trimming the number will deliver a more streamlined Parliament and significantly reduce its cost to the taxpayer. What's more, a Conservative government would close down Parliament's unaffordable pension scheme to any new members. Ministers would feel the pinch too, with a 5 per cent pay cut (and pay for ministers would be frozen at this level for the full term of parliament).

One of the most significant commitments, in terms of restoring integrity to Parliament, from the Conservatives is their pledge to have select committee chairs elected by backbenchers rather than appointed by whips – for more on this see the Constitutional Reform chapter. At an administrative level, the Conservatives have committed to placing limits on the number of 'special advisers' in government, and to returning to proper Cabinet-style government where decisions are made by the Cabinet as a whole rather than a select handful of ministers. The days of small cliques making the big decisions has to end. The Conservatives will see that it does.

Restoring trust is also about openness and engagement. That's why David Cameron has sought, at every opportunity, to engage with the public through his 'Cameron Direct' events – where he travels to towns and cities around the country to answer people's questions directly and in person – and that's why he has committed to continuing these events if he becomes Prime Minister. Talking about openness and engagement isn't enough; you have to demonstrate it. And David Cameron will.

Finally, it is worth pointing out that restoring trust and honesty is, to a certain degree, a matter of style when it comes to government. Gordon Brown's style is all about misdirection and indeed even dishonesty. We saw it with the 10p tax rate, we saw it with his promise of a 'zero per cent rise', and we saw it over spending cuts when he dubbed Cameron 'Mr Ten Per Cent' at the same time as leaked Treasury documents showed Brown was planning 10 per cent cuts of his own. Cameron's style on the other hand is all about honesty and transparency. You can see that in the party's plans for everything from the NHS to dealing with crime. But you can also see it in the manner Cameron conducts himself, whether by acknowledging when mistakes have been made – as was the case when he apologised for Section 28 – or when he risked public backlash by making clear that he didn't believe setting a pull-out date for Afghanistan.

Both in style and substance the Conservative Party is the only party which can restore trust and honesty in British politics.

30 reasons to vote Conservative

1. Delivering effective banking and financial regulation by empowering the Bank of England and scrapping Labour's discredited tripartite regulatory system.
2. Lowering tax on business and cutting away unnecessary regulation.
3. Cutting unnecessary spending and embedding a culture of productivity in the public sector.
4. Reducing the number of MPs by 10 per cent, cutting and freezing the pay of ministers and doing away with Parliament's unaffordable pension scheme for MPs.
5. Requiring anyone on jobseeker's allowance for more than two years to carry out community work in return for their benefits.
6. Creating 100,000 new apprenticeships and fully funding the existing 77,000 apprenticeships.
7. Creating an extra 10,000 university places to ensure that universities can meet demand.
8. Giving teachers the power to deal with disruptive pupils.
9. Empowering parents and other groups to set up their own schools when they aren't satisfied with the ones already available.
10. Delivering real-terms increases in NHS spending year on year.
11. Enabling the NHS to focus on patient outcomes by removing Labour's process-based targets.
12. Allowing people to join the general practice they want to regardless of location) and ensuring they can change to a new practice if they're not happy with their current one.
13. Tackling hospital infections by building 45,000 more single

hospital rooms and penalising hospitals when patients contract infections during treatment.

14. Blocking the construction of a third runway at Heathrow.

15. Constructing high-speed rail links across the UK.

16. Reducing our dependence on high-carbon energy sources by empowering households and businesses to generate some of their own electricity.

17. Protecting rural services such as family doctors and post offices.

18. Supporting farmers by requiring the public sector to buy British produce wherever possible.

19. Guaranteeing that the British people will have a referendum any time the government wants to transfer more power to the EU.

20. Holding an immediate strategic defence review to ensure Britain is equipped to deal with the challenges it now faces.

21. Repairing the Military Covenant, which has been all but destroyed by Labour.

22. Guaranteeing that international aid is delivered using a results-based approach.

23. Defending civil liberties by scaling back the surveillance state.

24. Helping families stay together by removing disincentives to cohabitation in the benefits system.

25. Recruiting 4,200 new health visitors to support families with young children.

26. Capping immigration from outside the EU and creating a dedicated UK Border Police Force.

27. Empowering police to deal with crime by doing away with Labour's forest of red tape.

28. Taking a zero-tolerance approach to knife crime.

29. Creating elected police commissioners to ensure the public can hold police to account.

30. Taking away the power of local councils to spy on local residents for spurious reasons.

About the author

Shane Greer is one of the UK's leading Conservative bloggers and commentators, appearing regularly on television and radio, including Sky News, BBC News, Daily Politics, BBC Breakfast, BBC World Service, Channel 4 News, More4 News, Al Jazeera and BBC Radio. He has blogged for the *Daily Telegraph* and the Centre for Policy Studies, and writes for the *Yorkshire Post*. He is the executive editor of *Total Politics*, a non-partisan political lifestyle magazine which he launched with Iain Dale.

Previously he was executive director of the Young Britons' Foundation – an organisation that trains conservative-minded young people in political technology such as campaign management, candidate development and television technique. During his tenure he rebuilt the organisation after several years of inactivity and revitalised its fundraising operation. Whilst at YBF, he was also a lead presenter on 18 Doughty Street Talk TV, the UK's first political internet television channel.

He is a judge in the annual Reed Awards in the United States, which recognise campaigning excellence across the spectrum of political campaigns.

Shane has a degree in law from the University of Liverpool and a master's degree in international law from the University of Glasgow.